SAFE AT SCHOOL

Awareness and Action for Parents of Kids Grades K-12

Carol Silverman Saunders

SAFE AT SCHOOL

Awareness and Action for Parents of Kids Grades K-12

Carol Silverman Saunders

Edited by Pamela Espeland

Free Spirit
PUBLISHING

Dedication

To Bob, Lauren, and Mitchell

Acknowledgments

Special thanks to Judy Galbraith, Pamela Espeland, Bert Holtje,
John Hopton, George Butterfield, Peter Blauvelt, and all the wonderful,
helpful people at the organizations listed in this book.

Library of Congress Cataloging-in-Publication Data
Saunders, Carol Silverman
   Safe at school : awareness and action for parents of kids grades K–12 / by Carol
Silverman Saunders.
      p.   cm.
   Includes bibliographical references and index.
   ISBN 0-915793-71-7
   1. Schools—United States—Safety measures. 2. School accidents—United States—
Prevention. 3. School violence—United States. I. Title.
LB2864.5.S28 1994
371.7'7—dc20   94-7165
                                                                                                          CIP

10 9 8 7 6 5 4 3 2 1
Printed in the United States of America
Cover and book design by MacLean & Tuminelly
Index compiled by Eileen Quam and Theresa Wolner

Some of the information on sexual harassment in Chapter Seven has been adapted
from *Sexual Harassment and Teens: A Program for Positive Change* by Susan Strauss with
Pamela Espeland (Free Spirit Publishing Inc., 1992). Used with permission of the
publisher.

Free Spirit Publishing Inc.
400 First Avenue North, Suite 616
Minneapolis, MN 55401-1730
(612) 338-2068

Contents

*"In our species, it isn't so much
the survival of the fittest
as the survival of those with the fittest parents."*

ELLEN GOODMAN[1]

1

Unsafe at School

▼ ▼

On Mother's Day, 1990, while driving home from grandma's house, we saw fire engines racing toward my children's elementary school in Greenburgh, New York.

When we got home, our phone was ringing. "Seely Place is on fire!" screamed my friend. She lives across the street from the school and was witnessing the desperate attempts of the fire squad to put out a huge fire in our *circa* 1910 school.

By the next day, we knew the bad news: Although no one had been hurt, our school was severely damaged. The children would not be able to return to it for a long time. They would have to attend classes for months in makeshift rooms at other schools around town. The eventual emotional toll on the children was enormous.

We also heard some frustrating, disturbing news: The cause of the fire was the school's ancient electrical wiring, which ignited inside a wall in my

1

daughter's first grade classroom. The same classroom that held her desk, her stuffed bunny, her own box of crayons, and the first book she ever read all by herself. *The same classroom in which for the past two years parents and teachers smelled something burning, yet the few times the custodian looked at the wall he found no major problem.* And now that classroom and several others were destroyed.

This was a perfect example of what safety experts mean when they say, "There is no such thing as an accident. There is always a warning." School administrators should have heeded the warnings from parents. And if parents had known how to get that smell investigated properly, the fire never would have happened.

That's when this book took shape in my mind. I envisioned a parents' school safety manual.

Parents need a way to be heard about their safety concerns in schools and to hold schools accountable for safety. As a parent who is obviously interested in safety, you probably started childproofing your house even before your first child was born. Now that your children are attending school, it's your responsibility to make sure their schools are safe, too. Why? Because, in ideal situations, all aspects of safety are monitored by various people in the administration. But in less than ideal situations, safety takes a back seat. As a concerned parent, ultimately *you* are the one who has the most at stake in seeing that all aspects of school safety are properly addressed.

You need to know what to do if there is a safety problem you see and want acted upon, whether it's a funny smell, a bully tormenting your child, sexual harassment, students with knives, or overuse of pesticides. The more you know about how to identify and evaluate safety at your child's school, the better the chance that you might be just the person who could help avoid the tragedy of a fire, a stabbing, a memory of abuse, a fractured skull on the playground, or poisoning from lead in school drinking water.

How Unsafe Are Our Schools?

We usually think of our schools as being very safe. After all, they provide more supervision than many children have anywhere else. Some schools are truly as safe as any place on earth could be, but others aren't. In fact, the belief that any school is really safe is one of the illusions we foster in order to get up every day and function in society.

Violence, crime, and environmental problems are on the rise in many communities, and these ills extend into the schools. Children are at risk at school from many sources: students wielding weapons; decaying physical plants suffering from lax maintenance; environmental toxins; even their own dangerous behavior.

Statistics show that appalling numbers of students are victims of crimes and injuries at school. In 1992, over 770,000 injuries occurred in schools, injuries serious enough to need emergency room treatment and subsequent referral to the Consumer Product Safety Commission's Injuries in Schools data gathering program.[2] Over 9,000 fires occur annually in educational institutions, according to the National Fire Protection Association, and the figure is rising every year.[3]

▼ ▼

INJURIES IN SCHOOLS

There is only one formal information-gathering service in the country that collects information on injuries in schools: the Consumer Product Safety Commission (CPSC). It collects data on injuries occurring in schools that are treated in hospital emergency rooms and are, according to patients, product-related. This is a very narrow collecting process—any injury not related to a consumer product is not counted—but it still yields shocking figures: in 1992, 773,149 injuries were reported, up from 724,572 in 1991. Boys were almost twice as likely to be hurt than girls—509,000 as compared to 263,000.

Here is a list of the types of injuries occurring in schools recorded by the National Injury Information Clearinghouse, part of the CPSC, for 1992:

▶ strain, sprain: 245,759

▶ contusion, abrasion: 189,187

▶ fracture: 136,357

▶ laceration: 116,322

▶ dislocation (of bone or ligament out of socket): 15,843

▶ internal injury: 12,264

▶ concussion: 9,132

▸ puncture: 6,348

▸ foreign body (small object in body; for example, stuck in windpipe): 5,369

▸ hematoma (blood swelling): 4,915

▸ avulsion (tearing away of skin; as opposed to laceration): 4,391

▸ poisoning: 1,965

▸ dental injury: 1,304

▸ crushing: 1,048

▸ burn, chemical: 886

▸ burn, thermal: 733

▸ ingestion (to take into the body, as food): 613

▸ amputation (of limb/finger): 590

▸ hemorrhage: 531

▸ burn, scald (to burn with hot liquid or steam): 416

▸ radiation: 347

▸ anoxia (deprivation of oxygen, as from carbon monoxide or asphyxiation): 253

▸ nerve damage: 190

▸ electric shock: 150

▸ submersion: 106

▸ aspiration (inhaling fluid into the lungs, often after vomiting): 43

▸ burn, not specific: 36

▸ other: 17,465

▸ not stated: 586

These are just the physical injuries children suffer at school—and remember, the injuries on this list are all product-related. Not counted are the injuries caused, for example, by falling down stairs, getting into fights, or attacks by other students.

▼ ▼

In addition to suffering injuries in schools, students are victims of violence and crime. The National School Safety Center (NSSC) has been able to document from surveys and studies that over three *million* crimes occur in schools each year, and the number is rising. The Center, established by presidential directive to study school safety with Pepperdine University, works together with the U.S. Department of Justice and the U.S. Department of Education toward the goal of bringing a national focus to school safety.

Consider, also, the following:

▸ More than one million students report that they have avoided some part of their school building out of fear of an attack at least once during the school year.[4]

▸ Approximately 90,000 guns and 600,000 knives are taken to school every day.[5]

▸ Over one-third of all students know someone personally who has either been killed or injured from gunfire.[6]

▸ 11% of teachers and 23% of students have been victims of violence in or near their public schools.[7]

I know firsthand what it's like not to feel safe at school. My days attending Hawthorne Junior High School in Yonkers, New York, were full of fear. Even back then, twenty-five years ago, it wasn't safe to walk through the halls. I remember groups of students hanging around, waiting in corners and on stairwells to stick pins into anyone who dared to pass through "their" territory. Groups of girls would swoop down on other girls outside school and lift our skirts over our heads "just for fun" (back then, we were required to wear skirts to school every day). Drug dealers—my girlfriends' boyfriends—pushed marijuana into my face in the school yard, angry that I refused to buy their joints. They surreptitiously pressed pills into my palms; when I refused to accept them, they acted like it was my fault when the pills scattered on the concrete. Every day there were fist fights outside school—between boys and girls, between races, between bewildered friends. Police patrolled the streets around the schools, not on foot but in cars. They didn't dare crack their windows even an inch.

As bad as it was then, the problems are worse today. Now there are guns, knives, and other weapons that were unheard of in the 1950s and 1960s. The drugs are stronger now. The buildings are older. We know more about toxic materials (asbestos, lead) that should be removed from schools. And the hallways are even more dangerous.

▾ ▾

SIX WAYS CHILDREN CAN GET HURT AT SCHOOL— AND THREE WAYS SCHOOLS CAN PREVENT INJURIES

Basically, there are three ways children can get *physically* hurt at school:

1. The child does something to cause an injury. Examples are incorrect use of playground equipment, not following directions, or their own aggressive behavior.

2. The physical situation causes the injury. Examples are environmental toxins and lax or nonexistent maintenance.

3. Another person causes the injury. Examples are violent or criminal behavior of another student, and absent or inadequate supervision by staff.

Children can also get *emotionally* hurt at school. There are three ways this can happen:

1. The child can be a victim of verbal abuse by a staff member or bullying by a student.

2. The child can be sexually harassed by a teacher or other students.

3. The child can be discriminated against by students and/or teachers because of race, sex, religion, ethnicity, or some other reason.

There are three ways schools can prevent students from being injured, both physically and emotionally—and parents can help with all three:

1. Protection. Schools can prevent accidents with proper maintenance, supervision, and prevention policies.

2. Regulation. Schools can enact rules to be followed to prevent injury.

3. Teaching. Schools and parents can teach children how to stay physically and emotionally safe. Schools can teach conflict resolution and social skills to help kids be more sensitive to the safety and well-being of others.

▾ ▾

What Makes a School Safe?

School safety involves first and foremost an *atmosphere* of safety, a climate in which children feel comfortable and happy. Safe schools may have the same problems as the surrounding community, but they are addressed and remedied quickly. Safe schools have principals, teachers, and students who care. The buildings and grounds are well maintained. Discipline policy is well-known and respected, drugs and weapons are vigorously kept out, safety measures are taught and reinforced, and environmental toxins are tested for and eliminated.

Most importantly, there is a well-known and established way for students and parents to report people problems or physical plant problems. Kids feel safe because they know that if someone acts up, that someone will receive a consequence for his or her actions. If the faucet in the bathroom needs fixing, someone will fix it. Everyone has pride in the school, a sense of ownership.

"Safe schools have zero tolerance for fear," says school safety expert Peter Blauvelt.[8] In safe schools, children can concentrate on learning, not on staying safe or staying alive.

Being the Bad Guy

Everyone wants safe schools, but almost no one wants to be the "bad guy" who confronts schools and demands solutions to safety problems, especially if there is no established means to convey these messages. The lack of policy regarding parent involvement in these matters is most likely due to the fact that many schools still look at parents as obstacles, not partners.

The system just isn't set up to accept parent involvement. Even if it was, many parents are afraid to approach schools because of their own feelings of anger and hurt from their childhood school experiences. According to Nancy Berla of the National Committee for Citizens in Education, "Schools often send a not-too-subtle message that parents who come to school frequently to ask to see teachers, or spend a lot of time with their kids, are meddlesome or unable to 'let go.'"[9] This message is sent so that schools don't have to deal with the "time consuming" and "irritating" matters that parents bring up.

With the information in this book, parents will be empowered to approach principals and other administrators about safety, with confidence and the knowledge that they are doing the right thing.

Some people might say that an emphasis on partnering with schools on safety instead of on improving the curriculum is wrong. But I propose that parents and administrators working together to promote safety will lead to all kinds of other benefits in education.

Safe at School doesn't tell you how to help your children with homework, have a good parent-teacher conference, or improve your child's learning. You can find lots of good information about these things in other books about education. But this book *does* tell you how to make your school playground safer, what to do if gangs rule the bathrooms, how to find out if there is lead in your school's drinking water, what to do if kids are bringing guns to your schools, and much more. In looking into solutions to these problems, you will forge relationships and bonds with the school that can blossom into increased educational benefits for your children.

Talking to schools about safety is more productive than making suggestions or requests about the educational program. For example, if you say to a principal, "I want my child to have Mrs. Smith for fifth grade next year," you are directly challenging the very nature of the principal's work. If you say, "What can we do to help get the school tested for lead in the drinking water?," you are showing concern for your child's health *and* the school staff's. They don't want to drink leaded water either, even if eliminating the problem will mean an expensive solution. So, when you work to improve safety, you are benefiting the teachers as well as the students, and your concern will be appreciated. Everyone will be happier, and happy people make schools better.

In addition, once more and more parents decide to get involved in children's safety in school, schools will find it necessary to accommodate their demands in other areas as well. This can and will include selecting teachers, principals, and curricula. School-based management (SBM) teams in schools around the country are doing this already. Indeed, parents deciding that schools must listen to their ideas about safety and other matters is a contagious idea.

Aren't There Federal Laws about School Safety?

Unfortunately, not yet. But educational law is catching up with reality. "With or without the presence of a constitutional amendment or supporting case law, school districts have a professional and legal obligation to protect students and staff against foreseeable risks of harm," writes educator Jerry Maze.[10]

In other words, it pays for schools to act on violence and environmental safety concerns, because parents are suing schools and sometimes winning. In addition, teacher education programs are starting to include course work in school law as a preventive measure. Parents, in the absence of the same professional training about school law, should know how the courts are thinking, too. This book reveals some of that thinking.

As more and more school-related dangers develop and are identified, lawmakers are enacting laws against them. But even if there are laws, it's hard to find out about how they apply to you and how they affect your schools. *The best way to start is to ask to see your school's policy book.* Usually kept in a binder, it includes all of the written policies regarding any laws or mandates your district has already set up.

"Isn't that spying?" one mother asked me when I told her I was reading our school's policy binder. Reading school policy is far from spying; it is every parent's *responsibility*. Schools must allow policy to be known. Ideally, they should make it easy, even publicize its availability. *Safe at School* tells you about some of the ways parents can get involved in creating, changing, and expanding school policies.

Getting Started

Given the opportunity, parents want to be involved with school safety, even if they are busy with other aspects of life. This was discovered by the National Association of Elementary School Principals (NAESP) during an annual National Principals Hotline. The March 1992 hotline brought more than 1,300 calls by parents over three days to 137 principals answering the calls. As the NAESP's executive director reported in the association's newsletter, "The principals were advised to urge parents to speak with the principal of their child's school and to insist that parents should discuss their worries with school authorities and should continue to voice their concerns or go to a higher level if needed." The newsletter reported that a "substantial number [of parents] wanted to know how to become more active in their child's school" and also to know "how to keep children safe in school."[11]

According to Joseph Fernandez, former New York City Schools Chancellor, "the role of parents in the public schools of America has been drastically changed—but has never been more important. Yes, the traditional 'PTA Mom' is still needed: being a room mother, serving on fundraising committees, helping out at the Valentine's Day dance, bringing in 'PTA Pop' for Career Day. But there is a need now for a deeper, broader parental involvement, and it's an absolute must that the school systems of the country open their arms to let parents in, even to sharing the decision-making process. Not just because parents are more sophisticated than before and have a right to know, which they are and do, but because so many terribly complicated things are happening to our schools, and happening so fast, they *need* to be part of it."[12]

Indeed, schools *must* let parents get involved in more than bake sales and helping in the library. If schools resist, it is up to parents to educate the educators as to the benefits. And even if educators don't or won't see the benefits to parent involvement, they at least have to acknowledge that parents have a right to demand a safe school environment for their children.

▼ ▼

EIGHT WAYS TO GET INVOLVED IN SCHOOL SAFETY

1. Talk to your children. Ask questions about their day. Document (write down) the date, time, names, and specifics of any problems they have. Report to the school any serious or recurring problems. Keep copies of your notes for future reference.

Many times, just having discussions with your children can improve their safety at school. Knowing what to say and how to say it is important. You'll find many suggestions throughout this book about talking with kids about safety.

2. Visit the school. This includes scheduled teacher conferences as well as other times. Look at bathrooms, the cafeteria, hallways, grounds, etc.

3. Volunteer for a parent organization committee. This will give you a "reason" to see inside the school if your school makes visiting difficult at first.

4. Attend parent organization meetings to hear what's going on. Request evening or before-school meetings if work prevents you from attending daytime meetings.

5. Talk to other parents. Ask questions. Compare experiences.

6. Read your local newspaper for information about your schools. If there is a major safety problem, you'll see articles about bomb threats, false fire alarms, thefts, vandalism, gangs, etc. Newspapers also carry reports on the actions of the board of education and other school activities.

7. Form a safety advocacy parent group that meets regularly to discuss and address problems as they come up. For suggestions and ideas, see "How to Form a Parent Safety Group" on pages 12–14.

8. Introduce yourself to the principal, school district superintendent, and school board members. Do this even before you plan on trying to solve any problems. If you've developed a relationship with people that are able to help, you're way ahead of the game.

How can you meet administrators? The principal is easy. Because you are a parent of a child in the school, the principal should be eager to chat with you. Call ahead for an appointment—and be sure to read "The School's Point of View" on pages 18–20.

You might be able to meet the superintendent at a PTO or PTA meeting. To meet board members, attend a school board meeting (superintendents attend these as well), or ask a friend to introduce you if you don't know any of them personally. You'll find that most board members are parents just like you.

▼ ▼

How to Form a Parent Safety Group

This book describes many situations that you can decide to help rectify. But before you say or do anything, the best course of action is to form a parent safety group if there is not already one at your school. A group of parents with a commitment to improving safety can do a lot more than just one parent acting on his or her own.

Start by contacting the president of the PTA or other parent organization. Find out if there is a parent safety group in place. If there is, join it. If there isn't, tell the principal that you want to start one. Request permission to prepare a flyer to send home with the children. The flyer should describe the group and its purpose, ask parents if they want to join, and tell them who to contact.

When you have a list of interested parents, arrange an initial meeting at someone's home or at the school to discuss everyone's unique concerns. This is important, because if parents are going to get involved in school safety and health, we must learn to distinguish between important and trivial hazards. Allow everyone to air their concerns, listen respectfully, then ask for a group consensus on which issue to address first and how to handle the others—perhaps using a mutually agreed upon prioritizing process. When it comes to school safety, no concern is really "trivial," but your group can't fix everything and will need to agree on where to start.

At your meeting, ask a volunteer to take notes. Plan a regular meeting schedule, perhaps once or twice a month. Formulate an agenda with a list of safety problems in order of importance. Use this book as a guide. Pick one issue that the majority of parents agree to start with. Then:

1. *Research the background of the problem.* Are there laws or school policies that affect it? Perhaps there is a policy but it's too vague and needs supporting details. Has anything been done in the past to rectify this problem? Are there unknown or unenforced rules regarding this problem? Ask volunteers to call various district people for answers to these questions. You may have to call state or federal education departments. Another way to gather information is to visit other schools and compare their situation with yours.

2.	*Be patient while the research is being done.* Observe the situation. Document, in writing, any and all facts and occurrences regarding the problem. Is it getting worse? Better on its own? Bring up the problem with other parents not on the safety committee. What do they think about it?

3.	*At the next meeting, share the facts and opinions everyone has gathered.* Perhaps this information puts an entirely new light on the situation. That's okay. Be flexible.

4.	*Redefine the problem based on the new information.* Often, you'll find that the situation involves the community as well as the school. Contact community resources such as police, fire department, social services, alcohol and other drug treatment programs, medical services, and more.

5.	*Develop at least three possible solutions to the problem based on what you have learned.* Consider how these solutions will affect students, parents, teachers, and administrators. Try to look at the issue from each group's point of view.

6.	*Meet with the principal to discuss the three solutions.* Realize that limited funding combined with ambitious goals creates a need for compromise on both sides. Also be sensitive to what Joseph Fernandez calls "authority cramps"—the uncomfortable feeling principals have when relinquishing control.

7.	*Select one solution to enact.* Perhaps the principal can help. Maybe the board of education needs to get involved. Talk about a timetable and the specific people needed to solve the problem.

8.	*Carry out the solution.* This may take a short or long amount of time. Be patient.

9.	*Watch for how the solution works.* Make changes if needed. Write thank-you letters to administration people who helped.

10. *Be realistic if the problem doesn't go away immediately.* Meanwhile, pat yourselves on the back for doing such a great job. Remind each other that safe schools are everyone's right and responsibility. Start on a new project!

▼ ▼

SAMPLE SAFETY PROJECTS

▸ Set up a suggestion box in the school so that anyone at any time can suggest ways to improve safety and other issues.

▸ Write and distribute a safety newsletter for parents and students.

▸ Start and add to a safety library on school safety topics to be housed at the school. To obtain material, contact the organizations listed on pages 203–207.

▸ Set up an easy-to-use system for students and parents to report safety concerns directly to the principal.

▸ Look into the environmental issues described in Chapter Eight, pages 139–158.

▸ Institute ways for parents to have more physical access to the school—a parents' room or corner of an office, parent safety patrols, a maintenance committee.

More advanced projects can be tackled after your group has had success with smaller goals. Throughout this book, you will find ideas for these, ranging from violence and crime deterrents, to investigating and influencing policy statements, to purchasing new playground equipment, to school bus safety improvements and much more.

▼ ▼

What to Do If You Meet Resistance

What if all attempts by your group to influence safety through the proper channels via the principal, superintendent, and school board are not being heard? According to school safety expert Peter Blauvelt, you are then entitled to go public. "Enough is enough," he insists. "Educators must stop repressing parent's safety concerns."[13] Going public means contacting the media (newspapers, local television stations, radio stations). Realize that this will most likely bring astonishingly fast results, although possibly damage relationships.

For example, a PTA in a violent school in Brooklyn organized a total school boycott (all the students stayed home from school) after a student was stabbed in the cafeteria. The boycott made the news, and the board of education met all of the PTA's demands: magnetic door locks, extra security guards, an additional lunch period to relieve overcrowding, more bilingual guidance counselors.

A parent in Greenwich Village called in the media when the school wouldn't acknowledge or remedy a problem with excessive dust (and suspected lead and asbestos) and debris during renovations. The mess was tested and cleaned quickly, but the mother and others were angry that they had to go this far to get action.

Let's get administrators to listen to us *before* a scandal is created and *before* tragedy strikes. It's in everyone's best interests—schools, administrators, parents, communities—to do so.

Funding for Safer Schools

"We ought to make every school the safest place in our society again."

PRESIDENT BILL CLINTON[14]

In his bill on educational standards, President Clinton supports the goal of schools that are free of drugs and violence. President George Bush talked about safer schools in his "America 2000" plan to improve schools. Lots of other legislators talk about these goals, too. Who wouldn't want safer, peaceful, environmentally sound, drug-free schools? It's very easy to say you are for these things, but it's harder to actually do something about them.

School funding comes from a complicated web of federal, state, and local money, although schools are currently financed mostly by local property taxes. Whether schools *should* be funded mainly by local taxes, or by some other more equitable means, is a subject our nation is grappling with right now. There are school-financing lawsuits currently pending in many states that aim to change the way schools are financed.

It does seem unfair that some public school districts spend only $3,000 per year per pupil and sometimes less, while others spend three or four times as much. This disparity can happen because school financing is a function of property taxes. Wealthy homes and/or industry mean more money per student.

But as the *New York Times* reported in 1993, "Proposals to do away with local school taxes altogether, replacing them with a state tax that could be apportioned equally among the schools, are almost uniformly dismissed around the country as undermining local control."[15]

In any case, there are many people who claim there is proof that redistributing money won't make schools any better or safer. A column in the Newark *Star-Ledger* titled "The Monied Path is a Dead End to Better Schools" argued that "No court decision in the last 23 years of endless litigation has yet offered helpful advice as to how to improve schools, just how to equalize spending."[16] It's true that more equalized spending *could* result in safer schools, as long as the money was earmarked for new roofs or additional security guards, for example. But spending on safety is hard to justify when, for example, new textbooks are needed just as much or even more.

Indeed, money that is spent on safety sometimes seems to the public like money that should have been spent on "pure education" (textbooks, supplies, teachers). When New York City Mayor David Dinkins announced a plan to spend "$28 million for 140 extra security guards, new X-ray machines and metal detectors that would allow daily weapons screenings at 20 high schools and less frequent screenings at 20 others,"[17] many people criticized him, saying that the city could not afford this much spending on safety.

Just how much should be spent on school safety? No one has added it up. But here's a way to look at total school spending as it compares to the rest of the federal budget. Joseph Fernandez points out that in 1992 the United States Secretary of Education requested nine billion dollars for America's 84,000 schools. This seems like a lot of money until you realize that the total federal budget is $1.45 trillion, so the administration was allocating *"less than one percent* of the taxpayer's money to their embattled schools." Fernandez goes on to note that the Persian Gulf war cost more than $45 billion, the savings-and-loan mess cost $290 billion, and the Pentagon's proposed budget for 1992 was $290 billion, or about thirty times what was to be spent on schools.[18]

Certainly our schools are worth a larger percentage of our national budget—but many voters don't think so. They all too often vote against school budgets and referendums, sometimes because they think this money will only fatten the wallets of administrators. In fact, in 1992 a town on Long Island awarded a $960,000 retirement package to the superintendent of a school district, triggering a legal challenge and public outcry. Sometimes too much money *does* go to fatten administrator's wallets.

But most of the time, the money is to be used, for example, to turn auditoriums into classrooms in overcrowded schools or to remove damaged asbestos and dangerous underground oil tanks. If you want safer schools, make sure to vote for your school budgets and encourage your friends to do the same. The tax cost to individuals is usually no more than $20 to $50 a year to finance these improvements.

Vouchers

School vouchers are a hot topic around the country. A voucher system of school funding would give money now spent for public schools to students who attend or want to attend private schools.

As with any controversial issue, each side has strong feelings. Proponents say that vouchers would make schools more competitive and therefore better. Opponents say that public schools would be destroyed if this money was taken away from them. They also think that the government should not subsidize religious schools, which many private schools are.

There are other arguments both for and against vouchers, too detailed to report here. Suffice it to say that many states are considering instituting vouchers—but note that in 1993 the state of California voted on Proposition 174, which would have instituted vouchers, and citizens voted against it.

School Boards and Funding

To make schools more accountable, school boards are supposed to issue documents showing where the money will be allocated in their yearly budget before the time comes to vote on it. If not enough money is being put toward school safety and is instead being used for questionable purposes, parents can organize to present suggestions for change to the board.

In 1992, some 50 Texas high schools purchased video equipment to help their athletic teams win games. This happened during a school funding crisis that ranked among the worst in the state's history.[19] If parents had been on the alert ahead of time, they might have been able to funnel those funds into, for example, lab safety improvements. If your school board is not issuing budget breakdowns, ask that they start as soon as possible. You'll find out more about how to monitor school board activity in Chapter Eleven.

Although many districts resist the idea of consolidating school districts, cutting administrative costs can save a great deal of money that can then be used to improve all aspects of schools, including safety. And more and more outside businesses are taking over management of schools and producing good results, so watch for more attention to be paid to this solution.

Parent Initiatives

Parents can help with funding in other ways, too. Look into corporate grants to schools. More and more business–school ties are being created, but the key is to know how to apply for grant money from large corporations. Find out if someone in your town is adept at grant proposal researching and writing, and ask if they would be willing to help by looking into grants that can improve school safety. Superintendents often have access to this information as well. There are grants for multicultural education, mediation programs, anti-gang activities, and more.

Meanwhile, parents are starting to organize to provide goods and services themselves to their schools to make them safer and healthier. Some people applaud this parent involvement; others label it unfair. As one opinion editor wrote in the *New York Times*, "What messages are we giving our children when, because of private donations, playgrounds in prosperous neighborhoods are upgraded and those in poor neighborhoods remain blighted by cracked pavement and rusting old equipment?" The answer to this is: There are plenty of parents in poor and underprivileged districts who have also contributed to and will continue to contribute to safer schools.

All parents have something they can offer. Those who are able to make private donations should not be discouraged. Those who don't have money to spare can contribute in other important ways—by donating their time, expertise, and commitment, for example. Don't let anyone tell you that you can't improve your school.

The School's Point of View

How do schools feel about parents trying to improve safety? Given a choice, many principals and other administrators would much prefer hearing parents' ideas about reducing crime or playground injuries than their complaints about teachers assigning too many worksheets. Criticize the worksheets and you're directly challenging the overall quality of education the school is trying hard to provide. Working with the school to improve safety doesn't challenge the educational program, and it helps administrators to solve one of their biggest problems. So we can probably assume that most schools will tolerate, if not always welcome, parent participation in safety issues.

Still, it helps to look at what you're trying to do from the other side of the school yard. The open-door policy that all good principals practice shouldn't be abused. Unless you have a life-threatening situation, don't burst into a principal's office full of anger. It's easy to get emotional when things affect your children, but it's best to cool off and take time to think first. You'll present your views better, and you'll be perceived in a more favorable light.

As mentioned earlier, it's often best to join or form a safety committee, develop a list of priorities, and arrive at a consensus on which issues to pursue before making any contact with the administration. If you make too many complaints or suggestions, none of them will be taken seriously and your power will diminish. Picture many parents approaching the principal with a variety of issues vs. one parent going in with one issue that many parents agree on. The first seems overwhelming to the principal; the second is likely to get attention because the one parent represents many.

Don't wait until a crisis is happening to establish yourself as a caring, involved parent. Develop relationships with as many school staff members as possible right at the beginning of each school year, so you can build on this good rapport later. Short notes and brief phone calls are all that is needed, if your work prevents you from making regular personal appearances on the school campus.

Realize that teachers and principals may be unsure of how to accommodate the new role parents are playing in school involvement, just as parents are unsure of how to accomplish it. Therefore, make sure to use the appropriate channels. A principal will not take kindly to parents going to the superintendent before talking to her or him directly. It's only common courtesy. Go up the chain of command from the bottom, and keep going up until the problem is solved.

It also helps to know a little about what principals think of parents, at least as reflected in the professional literature. Try to locate a few issues of *Principal* magazine and *The Executive Educator* (try your county library or the library of a local university or teachers' college). You might be surprised by what you find. In 1992, for example, there were articles published with the following titles: "Parents Say The Darnedest Things," "Whine Busters," and "Five Strategies for Managing Angry Parents." These articles and others—some conciliatory, some condescending—can give you valuable insights into what things look like from the principal's side.

Finally, there is the fear many parents have that if they speak up about controversial issues, their children will be subtly or overtly punished. This topic is almost taboo to talk about, but some brave parents have brought it up at occasional PTA meetings I have attended, and friends at other schools have mentioned it as well. Unfortunately, it *is* true that if you push too hard or make unreasonable demands, this *may* happen. It may even happen if you are being perfectly diplomatic. On the other hand, your child may be singled out for unfavorable treatment for other reasons as well, due to personality conflicts or poor communication skills.

In any case, it would be nearly impossible to prove that your child was being punished for your involvement, and it would be foolhardy to make any accusations for this reason. If you do suspect this is happening, back off a little or change tactics and see if this makes a difference.

I have included these thoughts here, even at the risk of sounding negative, because if I left them out you might not trust the other information in this book. However, this problem—punishing kids for their parents' involvement—is much less likely to manifest itself if good interpersonal skills are used and if parent involvement is based on good working relationships. Don't jump to the conclusion that any trouble your child may be having with a teacher or administrator is a direct result of your involvement as a parent concerned about school safety.

2

Violence and Crime
in Schools

▼▼▼▼▼▼▼▼▼▼▼▼▼▼▼▼▼▼▼▼▼▼▼▼▼▼▼▼▼▼▼▼▼▼▼▼

School is a part of society, and as society gets more violent, so do our schools. Only recently it has been said that children are being forced to attend schools in such violent surroundings that adults would never tolerate the same conditions in the workplace. Yet the workplace, too, is becoming a location where one is likely to be hurt or killed by disgruntled former employees or jilted lovers of present employees. We risk being victims of violence and crime 24 hours a day, wherever we are. It's a tragedy, especially when it comes to schools. Schools, like homes, should be safe havens, but they are not anymore. The problem seems to be getting worse, not better, and obstacles to improvement abound.

Schools can't cure all of society's ills. Parents are really the ones who should be responsible for their children, but as society changes, more and more students don't have parents they can count on to guide them. Experts agree that in order for schools to become less violent, parents, the community, and society in general must each play a large role.

Experts further agree that there is no one right way to deal with crime and violence in schools and society, but you'll find here some ideas on how you can keep your child's school as safe as possible.

Statistics on School Violence and Crime

Violence and crime no longer affect only inner city schools; today they are suburban as well as urban problems. A 1989 Justice Department survey showed that 3% of urban students had taken a weapon to school, as had 2% of suburban students. Twenty-four percent of urban students were afraid of attacks at school, as were 20% of suburban students. Eight percent of urban students said they had been victims of crime, as compared to a close 7% of suburban students.[1]

According to a survey by the National School Boards Association, 97% of school principals say that school violence has increased nationally in the past five years. However, 61% claim that the violence is increasing in districts other than theirs—a figure that some experts say indicates a lot of denial.[2]

Local surveys show a dramatic increase in weapons toting. For example, a June 1992 survey of 1,400 New York City students found that 20% took guns or knives to school.[3] Of that 20%, 68% believed that their families would want them to use those weapons to defend themselves. Clearly it's not enough to teach students to use methods other than weapons to solve problems. We must also educate their parents.

▼ ▼

FIND OUT MORE

For more information on all aspects of school violence and crime, contact the following organizations:

- National School Safety Center (NSSC)
  4165 Thousand Oaks Boulevard, Suite 290
  Westlake Village, CA 91362
  Telephone: (805) 373-9977

● National Crime Prevention Council (NCPC)
   1700 K Street, N.W., 2nd floor
   Washington, DC 20006-3812
   Telephone: (202) 466-6272

▼ ▼

Weapons in Schools

Why do children bring weapons to school?

▶   Because they think they need them to protect themselves.

▶   Because they believe their friends will think they are "cool."

▶   Because they intend to commit a crime.

Weapons that are prohibited by schools are defined as any items that are capable of causing harm or bodily injury and for which there are no educational or instructional purposes. In addition to guns and knives, school personnel have confiscated a horrifying variety of weapons: pen guns, pen knives, belt buckle blades, nunchakus, brass knuckles, dart guns, and even spud guns—guns that shoot potatoes instead of bullets.

Still other weapons are carried to school that are not against the law—yet. In 1993, the *New York Times* reported that in addition to bringing knives to school, students were planning to use boxcutters, razors, screwdrivers, army knives, and even forks as weapons.[4] All of these can be brought to school without fear because loopholes in anti-knife laws allow them to be carried. Boxcutters, utility knives, or wallpaper trimmers "could" be needed for that job after school; army knives "could" be needed for a scouting program. The article went on to say that kids are sneaking razors into school tucked into notebooks, clothing, even hairdos, and that hundreds of children across the country are killed, disfigured, and maimed each year with boxcutters and razors. Safety expert Peter Blauvelt responds: "All states have laws about concealed weapons and knives. But no matter what they are, school boards can say no to knives, including Swiss army knives and boxcutters."[5]

Many parents know their children are bringing weapons to school but look the other way because they want their children to be able to protect themselves. This thinking is wrong.

Guns in Schools

*"Recently, my five-year-old son was watching a TV
news broadcast about children bringing weapons
to school and wanted to know if he would have his
own gun by the time he went to school."*

LETTER TO THE EDITOR, *SESAME STREET PARENTS' GUIDE*[6]

We've gone from hearing about one isolated shooting at a school a year to one a day. In fact, over eleven children a day are killed by guns in the United States, and this number is rising. Most young victims are killed by friends, relatives, and fellow students, either accidentally or due to misunderstandings. Our country is in a youth firearm health crisis, and it's up to parents to stop it if the government can't.

In 1990, the Center to Prevent Handgun Violence (CPHV) issued a revealing report on the problem.[7] Called *Caught in the Crossfire: A Report on Gun Violence in Our Nation's Schools*, it was based on over 2,500 news stories. (CPHV used this method to collect data because currently there is no mandated reporting of gun violence in schools on a national level.) The report found that during the four years prior to the study, 71 people had been killed with guns in school, 201 had been wounded, and at least 242 had been held hostage by "gun wielding assailants." The incidents occurred in over 35 states, proving that guns in schools is a widespread problem. The report also found that high schools (63%) were not the only schools affected—junior high/middle schools (24%) and elementary schools (12%) were affected as well.

In order to rid our schools of guns, guns need to be better controlled in our society. The passage of the Brady Bill on November 10, 1993, is a first step. Named for former Presidential press secretary James Brady, who was shot during a 1981 assassination attempt on President Ronald Reagan, the bill requires a five-day waiting period and a background check on anyone who wants to buy a handgun. Many people feel that additional gun control laws will now be passed. "We need to get sensible, reasonable gun regulation passed in America, and people have got to speak out," said Attorney General Janet Reno at a U.S. Chamber of Commerce conference.[8]

▾ ▾

GUNS IN SCHOOLS: WHY, WHEN, AND WHERE

What are the causes of gun violence in schools? *Caught in the Crossfire* listed the following reasons in descending order of frequency:

▸ drugs/gangs

▸ longstanding disagreements

▸ playing with or cleaning guns

▸ romantic disagreements

▸ fights over material possessions

▸ depression

▸ vendetta against society

▸ racial hatred or bias

▸ name-calling

▸ vendetta against school employee

When does the violence happen? Again in descending order of frequency:

▸ between classes

▸ during class

▸ after school

▸ lunchtime

▸ athletic events

▸ commuting to and from school

▸ before class

▸ school carnival

▸ field trip

Where do shootings and hostage-takings occur? In descending order of frequency:

▸ hallways

▸ classrooms

▸   school grounds

▸   next to schools

▸   athletic facilities

▸   school buses

▸   school parking lot

▸   cafeteria

▸   restroom

▸   auditorium

In other words, our children can be victims of gun violence anywhere, anytime, for almost any reason.

▼ ▼

A more recent study from the Harvard School of Public Health reveals more alarming facts about kids and guns.[9] *A Survey of Experiences, Perceptions, and Apprehensions about Guns among Young People in America* is the first study about guns to cover "a cross-section of students in the sixth through twelfth grades in public, private, non-Catholic and Catholic schools in America." Between April and May of 1993, 2,508 students in 96 schools were asked questions "dealing with gun ownership, shooting at others, being shot at, being injured, being suspended, carrying weapons, carrying guns specifically, being physically threatened, and others." Some results:

▸   15% say they have carried a handgun on their person in the past 30 days

▸   9% say they have shot a gun at someone else

▸   11% say they have been shot at by someone with a gun in the past year

▸   22% say they would feel "safer" having a handgun on their person if they were going to be in a physical fight

▸   39% know someone personally who has either been killed or injured by gunfire

▸   59% say they could get a handgun "if I wanted one."

Further, only 56% of the students would like to abolish guns, while 27% would feel something was missing if guns were banned and 17% aren't sure. Seventy-five percent of the students agree that "because many young people know where to get guns, violence and danger for young people has increased."

Any gun incident occurring at school must be immediately reported to the police by the principal, even if no one was hurt. However, as you'll discover in "Reporting School Crime" on pages 39–41, there are many reasons why schools may be reluctant to report such incidents.

There is a law that makes it a federal crime to carry firearms onto school property. The Gun-Free School Zone Act was signed into law in 1990 by President George Bush. It prohibits the possession or discharge of a firearm within 1,000 feet of any school. (Exceptions include law enforcement officers and people living in homes located within 1,000 feet of schools.) The penalty is up to five years' imprisonment or a fine of up to $250,000 or both. While this law is commendable, many experts say it's not creating enough of a deterrent due to lack of publicity and enforcement.

A report by the Center to Prevent Handgun Violence titled *Kids Carrying Guns* describes many loopholes in gun control laws that prevent police from having the authority to stop teenagers who are openly carrying firearms.[10] In particular, Arizona, Kansas, and Colorado were found to have lenient laws allowing minors to carry and possess guns. The report found that "although many states limit carrying of *concealed* weapons, the majority of states fail to ban the *open* possession of handguns by all persons under 21." Also, "Only 13 states and the District of Columbia directly prohibit all minors under 21 from openly carrying handguns." And, "There is no federal prohibition on open carrying or possession of handguns by minors."

Senator Daniel Patrick Moynihan (D-New York) argues that since the federal government already controls the manufacture of bullets through licensing by the Bureau of Alcohol, Tobacco and Firearms, it should also get involved in bullet control. "Our country has a two-century supply of guns," he points out, "but there is only around a four year supply of bullets."[11] Moynihan compares this to government involvement in automobile seatbelt regulation. Back in 1960, no one thought cars were a public health problem; eventually many safety features were mandated by government. Since gun violence is now a public health problem, bullets and other ammunition such as cartridges should be controlled as well.

▼ ▼

GUNS AND THE NRA

The National Rifle Association (NRA) believes that every American has the right to bear arms, and that right is protected by the Second Amendment to the Constitution. Gun control advocates believe that the NRA has misinterpreted the meaning of the amendment and that the framers of the Constitution had no intention of allowing guns to proliferate as they have now.

The NRA has a pamphlet that it sends to parents who request it. Called "A Parent's Guide to Gun Safety," the pamphlet gives little information about the proper storage of guns and ammunition in the home. It makes no mention of the laws in many states that make it a crime for parents to fail to store guns properly. Rather, it discusses at what age children should be taught how to use guns.

The NRA offers a gun safety program for kids called "Eddie Eagle." The program is taught and represented by a person dressed in an eagle costume. Many people believe that this program sends the message to children that guns are fun. If "Eddie Eagle" is being offered in your school, it should be carefully monitored. As a parent concerned about guns in schools, you might want to try to replace the NRA program with the STAR curriculum created by the Center to Prevent Handgun Violence; see pages 30–31. Or, if you can't replace "Eddie Eagle," at least try to get your school to offer both programs—and plenty of opportunities for discussion among parents, teachers, and students.

▼ ▼

What You Can Do about Gun Violence

As a parent, you *can* do something about the horrifying trend of gun violence among young people, on the streets and in our schools. Here are six suggestions you can start implementing today:

1. *Follow the urging of the American Academy of Pediatrics and other gun control advocates and do not keep a gun in your home at all.*[12] Studies have found that the likelihood of the gun being used against you by an intruder is higher than the likelihood of you defending yourself with it.[13]

The *New England Journal of Medicine* reported in June 1986 that the risk of being killed by a gun was nearly triple in homes with guns than in homes without them.[14] A good alarm system is a better way of protecting your family, and alarm systems are becoming more affordable all the time. As another incentive not to keep a gun around, homes with guns have higher suicide rates.[15]

2. *If you must own a gun, store it unloaded in a locked container, carry the key with you, and store the ammunition in a totally different place.* More and more states are making this the law rather than just common sense.[16]

The following states have laws making it a crime to leave a loaded firearm where children can gain access to it: Florida, Iowa, Connecticut, Virginia, Maine, California, New Jersey, Wisconsin, Maryland, and Hawaii. In addition, the following cities have passed laws related to guns and kids: Elgin, Illinois; Houston, Texas; and Baltimore, Maryland. Contact your local police department for information about the laws in your city and state.

3. *Teach your children to **don't touch, leave the area, and tell an adult** if they ever encounter a gun.*

4. *Ask the parents of your children's friends if they have guns in the home and, if they do, how the guns are stored.* If there are guns around, no matter how the parents say they are stored, you might want the children to play at your house instead. Children cannot always be relied on to follow the "don't touch" rule. And even if your children follow it, what if their friends don't?

5. *Find out if a gun safety curriculum such as STAR, offered by the Center to Prevent Handgun Violence, is being offered in your school.* Request that it be offered if it is not. Be leery of the "Eddie Eagle" gun safety curriculum from the National Rifle Association (see page 28).

6. *Consider forbidding your children to play with toy guns.* While it is true that children will "create" guns from almost any toy, it is not necessary to hand them lookalikes of killing machines. The same goes for cigarettes and alcohol. Letting children play with toy cigarettes and/or pretend to "get drunk" is not appropriate if you want to discourage smoking and drinking.

What about guns that are obviously toys? There have been reports of problems with the giant, fluorescent-colored "super-soaker" water guns; for example, when a child squirts someone, that person takes offense and responds with shooting or other violence. As a concerned parent, you may want to take a stand against guns of *any* kind in the home—real ones, toy guns that look real, even toy guns that don't look real.

7. *Call your legislators to tell them that you support gun control legislation.*

▼ ▼

PREVENTING GUN VIOLENCE WITH STAR

The Center to Prevent Handgun Violence (CPHV) has developed a curriculum for preventing gun violence called STAR ("Straight Talk About Risks") for grades pre-K through 12. Here are descriptions of two activities contained in the curriculum:

▸   "Understanding Media Violence" (for grades 3–5). Students brainstorm a list of favorite TV shows, movies, songs, and video games, and identify characters in them that use guns to solve problems. In small groups, students create ideas that are alternatives for these characters. The class then talks about the differences between media and real-life violence, and about how the lack of information about alternative means to solve problems leads people to use guns.

▸   "Discussion of the Misunderstood 2nd Amendment" (for grades 9–12). Students discuss information about the Second Amendment provided by the CPHV. They imagine that they are delegates to a constitutional convention to reconsider the Bill of Rights and decide if they would adopt the Second Amendment today.

A CPHV survey found that of 40 textbooks studied, half were incorrect or ambiguous in their presentation of the Second Amendment.[17] The Second Amendment to the United States Constitution reads: "A well regulated Militia, being necessary to the security of a free state, the right of the people to keep and bear Arms, shall not be infringed." Gun control advocates say that this amendment was added only to protect the rights of each state to keep a militia, *not* to guarantee the right for all people to keep and bear arms.

For more information about CPHV and STAR, write or call:

- Center to Prevent Handgun Violence
  Education Division
  1225 Eye Street, N.W., Suite 1100
  Washington, DC 20005
  Telephone: (202) 298-7319

CPHV is chaired by Sarah Brady, wife of James Brady. You can also contact this organization to find out about gun control in general, and about specific gun control laws in your state.

▼ ▼

Preventing School Violence and Crime

Open vs. Closed Campuses

High school students want the freedom to go where they want at lunchtime. They want to eat Big Macs, maybe catch some rays, see a friend who has graduated. "Open" campuses allow students this freedom, but due to safety concerns, more and more high schools are "closing" their campuses not only during lunchtime but for the entire school day.

"Schools that are working on improving safety either are already 'closed' or are talking about the need to be 'closed,'" says George Butterfield, deputy director of the National School Safety Center (NSSC). Unfortunately, many schools become "closed" due to tragic circumstances—because students died in car crashes, or were involved in drug and alcohol offenses or crime and violence during off-campus lunch excursions.

"Closing" a campus is one of the most inexpensive, effective safety measures a school can take, and it's not necessary to wait for a crisis. Like many safety measures, this one can prevent problems from happening. However, there is often a lot of opposition to "closing" a campus, mostly if there have been no problems yet. Students don't want freedoms taken away—they want more added! "Traditionally, high school campuses have been 'open,' and people think it's a big deal to 'close' them. What we now know, however, is that once it's done, it's not a big deal, and everyone adjusts very well," Butterfield explains.

If you'd like to bring this issue to your school safety committee, be prepared to discuss the pros and cons.

Problems caused by "open" campuses include:

▶ Non-students can enter the campus and cause security problems.

▶ Students can be victimized or hurt off campus.

▶ Contraband can be brought back to school.

▶ If the school uses student ID's, students must be carded again, using up time.

▶ It can take too much time for students to return to class, and they can cause interruptions when they come in late.

▶ If a school wants to institute weapons checks, the school can't be "open."

Problems caused by "closed" campuses include:

▶ Not many!

The main drawback appears to be one of where the students will eat lunch. The food service may have to be expanded or changed. Maybe healthy "fast food" can be invited into the lunch program, or perhaps fresh salads and other appealing foods can be added. Lunch may have to be changed to shifts, but this is often a benefit because it eases cafeteria overcrowding.

If you meet resistance in proposing a "closed" campus, you may want to suggest a compromise: The campus will be "closed" for all students except seniors, or for all students except seniors in the last six months of their senior year.

What if your child's campus is "open" and you don't want to or can't change the system, yet you are concerned about your child's safety? Talk to your child about the issues described in this section. Insist that he or she eat lunch on campus, and perhaps offer an occasional reward to make up for the fact that "everyone else" gets to go off-campus.

Metal Detectors

Experts are divided on the value of using metal detectors to confiscate guns and knives that students try to bring into schools. Districts that decide to use them usually don't buy one for every school; instead, they rotate one or more among various schools. Besides saving money, this approach works because students don't know what day the metal detector is going to be at their school. It takes them by surprise.

Detractors say that metal detectors are too time-consuming and labor intensive, and besides, they don't alleviate feelings of aggression and violence. In addition, many claim that metal detectors don't work, as evidenced by the striking numbers of murders and attacks committed in schools where metal detectors have been in place. "All bets are off after the initial screening," Peter Blauvelt explains. "It's not like a school is an airplane up in the sky. A lot can happen in six hours—weapons can be smuggled into schools through windows, during outside gym, and during fire alarms."[18] Blauvelt feels that metal detectors give schools a false sense of security.

What if a student refuses to undergo an entry search through a metal detector? "Technically, students can't refuse because students can't make the choice not to go to school under compulsory education laws," says George Butterfield.[19] He is surprised that there has not been much attention paid to this issue.

Searches

Another aspect of controlling school violence and crime is the battle between the need to maintain order and the issue of student privacy. Public schools are allowed to do locker searches and other searches that would be considered an invasion of privacy if they occurred outside the school. Because schools are still somewhat *in loco parentis* (acting in place of the parent), they can search a locker on a strong suspicion of drugs. Some students (and their parents) feel that it is a violation of their rights to be searched in school.

Schools must be able to act to make school safe for *all* students. While some parents might claim, "Don't touch my kid," this attitude is dangerous. Next time it might be a search of another child that turns up a weapon meant for yours.

Searches of desks and lockers are generally allowed by federal and state laws. Students must be told in advance that the lockers belong to the school, not to them, and that the school may check lockers. According to the National School Safety Center (NSSC), distributing district-owned locks or requiring that students use only locks for which the school has combinations can enhance the school's position regarding the right to search. George Butterfield notes that "if students put their own locks on their lockers, that heightens the feeling of privacy, so schools should issue school locks."[20]

Searches of personal possessions are also allowed and may include book bags, jackets, pockets, pocketbooks, and vehicles. Schools may use devices such as metal detectors, video and audio equipment, and other means of locating contraband.

An adult witness should always be present during a search—a male when a male student is searched, a female when a female student is searched. Every attempt should be made not to embarrass the student. Strip searches are not allowed, as they violate decency. As reported by the National Education Association, "With only two exceptions, the courts have held that strip searching students violates the Constitution."[21]

For more information on searches, see *Parents, Schools, and The Law* by David Schimmel and Louis Fischer (Columbia, MD: The National Committee for Citizens in Education, 1987).

Bomb Threats

Caller ID, available in limited areas, can cut down on the problem of bomb threats. This service records each caller's phone number on a screen and stores it for retrieval.

A bomb threat is a form of terrorism and should never be treated as a joke. Some schools institute special codes to announce bomb threats over the loudspeaker so children are not alarmed. Then the school can be evacuated quickly and calmly.

Beepers

Beepers have become a popular way to keep in touch, but they've also become a controversial issue where school safety is concerned. Drug dealers and gangs use them so much that having a beeper has become synonymous with being involved in illegal activity.

But what if parents wants to equip their children with beepers for safety? In some states, California being one of them, they are out of luck because beepers have been outlawed. Anyway, schools don't like beepers, and it's not just because of their nefarious reputation. It is impossible to teach when students' beepers are constantly going off during lessons.

If parents and students truly need beepers for some reason before and after school, the beepers can be checked in and held for safekeeping at the school office during the day. If anyone, including a parent, needs to contact a student for legitimate reasons, all they have to do is call the school office and the student will be summoned to the phone. Some schools allow beepers for medical reasons, but these need to be approved in writing by the principal.

Personal Defense Devices

"Most states allow people to carry Mace [tear gas] and other devices like pepper spray and sound-emitting gadgets, but schools must say no these, too, including for teachers," Peter Blauvelt says.[22] New York and Wisconsin ban personal defense sprays, and special permits are required in California and Massachusetts. Experts claim that self-defense sprays that shoot tear gas or hot pepper may give people a false sense of security because attacks are usually so sudden that victims don't have a chance to use them.

What's happening in schools is that the sprays are being misused and sprayed in the halls. A school in Newark had to be evacuated when someone stole another student's spray and released it in the hallway. Twenty-nine people were hospitalized for headaches, nausea, coughing, vomiting, and shortness of breath.[23] Safety experts say this is happening frequently around the country. Sprays carried for protection are being abused. Most likely, the students in the Newark school either were curious about the effects of the spray or were not aware of how dangerous sprays can be. In situations where police have used pepper sprays instead of guns to subdue suspects, people have died due to reactions from asthma or cardiac conditions or complications from alcohol or drug-related conditions.

While personal defense sprays are certainly preferable to guns, they have no place in a school setting either. Ask your school to ban them if it hasn't already.

Conflict Resolution

The most exciting prospect for preventing and even eliminating violence in schools comes from conflict resolution programs. These programs, which include peer mediation and can also extend to teacher–parent and teacher–teacher mediation, are currently in place in almost 5,000 schools, according to Annette Townley, Executive Director of the National Association for Mediation in Education (NAME).

What makes these programs work? "They are places where honesty, respect, and listening can occur," says Townley.[24] NAME, a leader in the growing field of conflict resolution and violence prevention, claims that mediation can reduce school discipline problems, improve attendance, reduce violence, increase thinking skills, and create respect for diversity.

What is the key to mediation's success? It assumes that conflict is a natural human situation that can be resolved with skills that can be learned. It holds that conflict doesn't have to be avoided; it must be dealt with, but not with violence. It helps students find ways other than violence to solve their disputes. This help is needed because many children have not been taught these skills. Indeed, movies and television programs give daily lessons in using violence to solve problems.

Peer mediators are not partial, nor do they place blame. They don't hand down judgments; they help troubled students work out solutions. "They are not a student court—no one is considered guilty or innocent," Peter Blauvelt explains. Mediation is better than traditional methods of dealing with discipline—such as suspension, detention, and expulsion—because it really solves problems instead of just doling out punishments. Since mediation is always confidential, it helps students preserve their dignity. In addition, the skills that students and teachers alike learn in mediation programs can be used for a lifetime.

Mediation programs can be difficult to initiate, and not only because they are expensive (the costs of hiring a trainer or training school staff can be high). It takes a lot of time to train the student mediators, and the school staff must devote considerable time and effort to support the program. But the schools that are taking the risk and making the investment agree that it's worth spending several thousand dollars to save students' lives.

For information on setting up mediation in your school, contact the National School Safety Center (see page 22) or:

- The National Association for Mediation in Education (NAME)
  University of Massachusetts
  205 Hampshire House
  Amherst, MA 01003
  Telephone: (413) 545-2462

▼ ▼

20 THINGS YOU CAN ASK YOUR SCHOOL TO DO TO PREVENT SCHOOL VIOLENCE AND CRIME

1. Provide additional surveillance for restrooms, whether by adults or surveillance cameras. Request that access be restricted; perhaps some bathrooms should be closed for part of the day. Some schools have eliminated separate staff bathrooms so that staff can use student bathrooms and thereby offer extra supervision.

2. Provide a checking area for coats and jackets.

3. Teach a curriculum that stresses nonviolence, especially in the younger grades. Experts say that if we don't catch violence-prone kids in elementary school, it's a lot harder to turn them around when they are older.

4. Institute parent patrols, receptionists, and/or challengers. Receptionists greet visitors and refer them to the office to register. Challengers are prepared to deny access to the school. Which is best? That depends on the school environment.

5. Control access to the school. Ask for doors that only open from the inside; alarms; new, more secure windows and doors; and closed-circuit television.

6. Bring in peer mediation. See "Conflict Resolution" on pages 35–36.

7. Provide school social workers and guidance counselors. These trained professionals can help students solve personal problems that otherwise might lead to violence.

8. Use metal detectors, if guns and knives are prevalent.

9. Institute student ID cards.

10. Develop a student bill of rights.

11. Hire securlty guards, or better yet, juvenile police officers. If these individuals are well-liked, students will be more likely to report crimes to them.

12. Conduct drop drills and drive-by shooting drills so students know what to do if gunfire erupts. Some schools are designating "safe rooms"—rooms without windows and with locks on their doors—that students can go to in the event of a gun threat or other danger.

13. Equip teachers with two-way communication devices so they can alert the office of an incident immediately. Parents can pitch in for two-way radios so the school can communicate faster with police and outside services, especially if phones go dead.

14. Establish a policy in which parents become financially liable for damage done by their children.[25] This is state law in some states.

15. Take attendance early in the day, every day. Institute a callback program if a student is absent without a call from a parent. If it seems like a good idea, take attendance more than once during the day.

16. Require that all visitors sign in and wear badges. While these practices in themselves won't stop all people who shouldn't be in the school from entering, it can, when combined with other security measures, create an atmosphere of alertness that might stop an intruder.

17. Consult with commercial security companies about other ideas to strengthen school security.

18. Ask police to patrol outside the school before and after school.

19. Publish a school safety and security handbook for staff and parents. You might volunteer to help with the writing, editing, and publishing process.

20. If the school is a polling place, ask police to patrol on election days. Ideally, voters should not have to walk through the school to get to the voting booths.

Reporting School Crime

"Educators and parents should have zero tolerance for fear events in schools, and parents should demand 100% reporting and analysis of violent events."

PETER BLAUVELT[26]

Effective crime prevention is the best way to reduce or eliminate crime in our schools, but setting up an effective crime reporting system is easier and can also lead to prevention. Since there is no national system in place to gather information on school crime, schools do not have an incentive to gather their own information, unless their state or county mandates it. (Parents could ask their legislators to mandate a national database on school crime and violence—a project for your parent committee?) However, if schools ignore crimes or fail to act on them, then students feel compelled to retaliate or to protect themselves, and "good" kids end up bringing weapons to schools.

Adding to this problem is the fact that schools have many reasons *not* to publicize violent events or call the police when there is a disturbance. George Butterfield and other experts offer these reasons why schools don't call police:

▶ They don't want to draw attention to themselves.

▶ They feel that they can take care of the problem.

▶ The administration doesn't understand the difference between an assault and roughhousing. They think that a major incident is really a minor one.

▶ The administration doesn't trust or like police.

▶ Calling the police takes too much time.

▶ They fear that they will be forced to do something about crime and violence problems on the school campus.

▶ They don't want bad publicity in the media.

▶ If they report all of the incidents, then principals may be blamed as the cause, so there is no incentive to be honest about it. "Superintendents and school boards transfer and fire principals for 'notoriety' in schools," Peter Blauvelt observes.[27]

▸ Teachers' unions can use a high crime rate to get salary increases that the administration doesn't want to give them.

▸ Teachers don't report incidents because they fear retaliation from students or they don't want to stigmatize an offender. Because of this, teachers' unions often report that crime is more prevalent than administrators state. Also, teachers are afraid to discipline students for fear of being sued. In fact, the courts usually, if not always, back discipline that follows guidelines established by the school.

▸ Schools don't consider themselves responsible for correcting violence and crime.

The solution to the nonreporting problem is for parents to demand total and accurate reporting of crime. The NSSC recommends that schools have a standard form students and teachers can use to provide complete and consistent information on accidents, discipline problems, vandalism, and security problems. The form should include where the event occurred, when, what happened, and who was involved. The form should be filled out immediately after the incident when details are easier to remember.

Parents should get involved in creating this form and rules regarding reporting, as should students and teachers. This way, everyone feels ownership of the rules and is more likely to understand and comply with them.

Many principals are afraid that if they notify parents of an incident, the parents will become angry and upset. However, parents get even angrier and more upset if they are *not* told about incidents, or if the principal minimizes the seriousness of a problem. Even if a principal doesn't have all of the facts yet, parents should be notified immediately in the form of a letter sent home from school.

When Should Schools Call the Police?

School behavior codes should clearly state the difference between school *misconduct* and school *crime*. The school should call the police when a crime is committed, not when misconduct occurs.

As defined by *The School Safety Check Book*, published by the NSSC,[28] school misconduct is student behavior that is unacceptable to administrators but does not violate criminal statutes. Absenteeism, tardiness, disrespect, bullying, inappropriate language, smoking, cheating, and lying are examples of misconduct. School crimes are acts defined as illegal by federal and state statutes or local ordinances, such as assault, vandalism, extortion, sexual offenses, and possession or use of alcohol, drugs, or weapons.

According to the NSSC, assault is the least understood crime occurring at schools. It is the difference between fights and assaults/battery that is the problem. An assault is a crime; a fight is a disciplinary infraction. While there is no legal definition of a fight, in school situations a fight means "mutual participation in an altercation,"[29] while an assault has at least one aggressor and one victim. Battery is defined as unlawful beating when an offender inflicts bodily harm on a victim. An assault includes jostling, tearing clothes, seizing or striking another.

Defining the difference between these disturbances is essential in order for a school to be as safe as possible. Police need to be called in at the right time, not too late, and not for minor infractions. "Police don't want to be called on a $5 theft out of a locker," George Butterfield explains.[30]

▼ ▼

VICTIMS' RIGHTS

Tell your children that they have a responsibility to learn and to do all they can to avoid being victims of a crime at school and anyplace else. However, if your child does become a victim, don't blame him or her. Make sure that every effort is made to discipline the party involved and to prevent the problem from occurring again.

In the past, it seemed like schools (as well as other parts of society) tried too hard to protect the rights of disruptive students and not hard enough to protect regular students whose learning environment was being invaded and whose safety was being threatened. This is changing now, and victims are demanding the rights they should have had all along. Here is some current thinking from *School Crime & Violence: Victims' Rights*, published by the National School Safety Center:[31]

Students and staff have a right to be protected against:

▶ foreseeable criminal acts

▶ student crime or violence which can be prevented by adequate supervision

▶ identifiable dangerous students

▸ dangerous individuals negligently admitted to school or placed in school, and

▸ school administrators, teachers, or staff who are negligently selected, retained, or trained.

If you feel that your child's rights have been violated at school, contact the NSSC or an attorney.

▼ ▼

Why Are Some Children Violent?

"Violence is learned, and we can teach children alternatives."

AMERICAN PSYCHOLOGICAL ASSOCIATION'S COMMISSION ON VIOLENCE AND YOUTH[32]

According to a report from the American Psychological Association's Commission on Violence and Youth,[33] parents play the largest role in affecting whether children are violent or nonviolent. The report, "Violence & Youth: Psychology's Response," identifies the following home life situations as high predictors of youth violence:

▸ parents who are sexually and physically abusive, antisocial, inconsistent, or who reject their children

▸ severe spousal fighting

▸ parents who mete out too-harsh punishments

▸ lack of supervision of children

▸ parents with criminal records

▸ youth access to alcohol, drugs, and/or guns

▸ hanging out with gangs, angry mobs, and other antisocial people

▸ doing poorly in school

▸ families in which generations have behaved the same violent way over and over again

▸ poverty—if there isn't enough money for the basics of life, it's a brewing ground for trouble.

The media bear a burden for fanning violent impulses. Most experts agree that watching violence on television contributes to violent behavior. "Television has great teaching potential. It's just been teaching the wrong things," the report points out. For example, in 1993, MTV's "Beavis and Butt-head" program was blamed for giving children ideas about starting fires and using illegal substances.

The report also mentions aspects of the school experience that contribute to violence, including:

▸ overcrowding (see Chapter Five, pages 90–91)

▸ heavy-handed and inflexible school rules (see Chapter Three)

▸ teacher hostility and lack of rapport with students

▸ inconsistencies in the limits of tolerance for student behavior.

Action to stop violence must start early in life, and parents, schools, and health professionals must all be involved. The report recommends programs that schools can use that teach social and emotional skills, like managing anger, negotiating, adopting another child's perspective, and thinking of alternative solutions to disagreements. While there is no way to make a place in school curricula for every social issue that needs to be addressed, priority can be given to life skills like communication, decision making, saying no, and conflict resolution; see pages 35–36.

Parenting for Nonviolence: What You Can Do

According to researchers, there are three key ways in which violent children err in their understanding of human relationships. These errors lead them to seek violent solutions or outcomes:

1. They don't look for the facts of a problem situation.

2. They think it is the other person who is being hostile.

3. They aren't able to think of nonviolent ways to solve problems.

There are three ways parents can help:

1. *Look for the facts.* Who was involved and why? Are there any facts missing? What might be the other person's point of view—his or her perspective on the problem situation?

2. *Understand that the other person may not feel as hostile as your child thinks he or she does.* Just because your child feels hostile doesn't mean the other person feels the same way, or to the same extent.

3. *Think of nonviolent solutions to problems and discuss them with your child.* For example, tell your child not to hit back if he or she is hit first. Instead, your child should get away and get an adult. See "Conflict Resolution" on pages 35–36 for information on how schools are instituting programs to offer alternatives to violence.

Involve your child in this process of coming up with nonviolent solutions. Many children, when they are not in the midst of a problem situation and all of the emotion it involves, are able to think clearly about alternatives to violence. Role-play problem situations and nonviolent solutions at home. This gives your child practice for the future.

▼ ▼

TEN MORE THINGS YOU CAN DO TO DISCOURAGE VIOLENT BEHAVIOR

1. Have rules about discipline in your home. Check out or buy a few good books about setting limits for children, read them, then try the suggestions you find. Be patient, be firm, be consistent, and don't expect miracles overnight. Here are two recommendations:

▸ *Discipline: A Sourcebook of 50 Failsafe Techniques for Parents* by James Windell (New York: Collier Books, 1991). Easy-to-implement strategies for staying in control.

▸ *How to Discipline Your Six- to-Twelve-Year-Old...Without Losing Your Mind* by Jerry L. Wyckoff, Ph.D., and Barbara C. Unell (New York: Doubleday, 1991). Another source of ideas that really work.

2. Teach kids that good manners can help ease tensions that can lead to violence. Pick up a children's book about etiquette. Recommendations:

▸ *Soup Should Be Seen, Not Heard! The Kids' Etiquette Book* by Beth Brainard (New York: Dell, 1992). For elementary school age children. A spiral-bound, easy-to-read (and fun) book on basic etiquette.

▸ *Social Savvy: A Teenager's Guide to Feeling Confident in Any Situation* by Judith Re with Meg F. Schneider (New York: Summit Books, 1991). For middle school and high school students. Covers all aspects of etiquette in an appealing way.

3. Be a good role model. Don't fight aggressively with family members. Don't support illegal activities, like buying stolen property or using illegal drugs.

4. Support the school's rules about violence and crime, and support the rules when they are enforced. Don't go into school angry when your child is disciplined. Find out the facts and be willing to admit when your child may have been wrong. On the other hand, support your child in telling the school his or her side of the story if you are reasonably sure that your child is innocent.

5. Don't let your children carry a weapon. See pages 23–31.

6. Tell your children not get to school too early or linger too long in the building after most people have gone home. See Chapters Four and Five for information on before-and-after school care and supervision.

7. Make sure that your children have constructive things to do after school. Suggestions: Clubs, sports, study groups, volunteer work, music lessons.

8. Keep the lines of communication open between you and your child. You're more likely to hear about problems and also to learn if your child is hiding out at a friend's house because he or she is afraid to go to school. Here are two books on communication that you may find helpful:

▶ *How to Talk So Kids Will Listen and Listen So Kids Will Talk* by Adele Faber and Elaine Mazlish (New York: Avon Books, 1980). A modern-day classic on communicating with your children.

▶ *Between Parent and Teenager* by Dr. Haim G. Ginott (New York: Avon Books, 1969). Sensible advice that has withstood the test of time. Dr. Ginott has also written *Between Parent and Child*, a guide to communicating with younger children.

9. If your child is the victim of or witness to a crime, consider counseling. Even if the child doesn't seem to be experiencing any problems now, post-traumatic stress syndrome is a possibility. This disorder may occur after a traumatic event and can include withdrawal, hyper-sensitivity, and constant reliving of the event.

10. Volunteer to get involved in school and community anti-crime projects. Show by your example that you care about crime and want to do something about it.

▼ ▼

Gangs: A Growing Problem

A gang is a group of people who have joined together, usually either to defend a turf area or for perceived protection from other gangs. Membership quickly leads to illegal behavior like stealing, shoplifting, mugging, fighting, underage drinking, doing drugs, and trespassing. Often members have to commit a crime in order to belong to a gang, as part of their initiation. Buying, selling, and using drugs are frequent requirements, as are carrying and using weapons. Gang members may die early or land in jail. *It can be hard, if not impossible, for a child to get out of a gang once he or she joins.* Preventing your child from ever entering a gang is of extreme importance.

According to the National PTA, pre-gang involvement frequently begins in elementary school.[34] It causes obvious personality and behavior changes. Children start avoiding family members and old friends. They stop participating in extracurricular activities. Tragically, gang involvement often can be linked to the lack of adult supervision, especially parental supervision.

Schools are recruiting grounds for gangs. Students can be actively recruited and coerced by gang members while in school or on the way to and from school. However, gangs are not merely a school problem; they are a community problem. It usually takes a coordinated effort by many community agencies to combat gang entrenchment. This can be made even harder because some communities deny that gangs exist in their area, either because they don't want to be branded by the media as "troubled" or because they really don't believe that gangs are active in their towns.

Some gangs are turf-oriented, some are not. A turf is an area that a gang decides belongs to them, and no one can pass through it without paying a price. A turf can be, for example, a particular school bathroom or a street corner. Gangs that are turf-oriented are likely to use violence to defend their area. More often than not, innocent bystanders are the ones who are hurt or killed.

In the past, females were only "mules"—they hid or transported weapons and drugs—but now they are full-fledged gang members. They are also frequent victims of gang violence.

Locking up the gang leader will not eliminate the gang; there are usually others members who quickly step in to lead.

A article published in the *New York Times* in 1993 reported that gangs exist in the suburbs as well as the cities, but that suburban gangs differ from urban ones.[35] They use baseball bats and golf clubs rather than guns and knives. They hurt, not necessarily kill. They commit crimes like stealing Mercedes Benz hood ornaments. Suburban gangs are "short-lived alliances" existing for as little as 48 hours. "Dissing," or offending another member of a gang, is what starts trouble, and that trouble is more often at school, not on the street.

The *New York Times* article further states that most gang members are attempting to escape from difficult family lives. Others have parents who are not exercising enough control over them. Law enforcement officials are amazed when parents of these children say, "How can you prove my kid had a gun?" instead of "My god, my kid has a gun!" They say, "Why did you pick up my child?," not "What was my 12-year-old doing out at 2 a.m.?" Police often try to contact the parents in the middle of the night and can't find them.

What can schools do to prevent gangs and gang activity? The National School Safety Center offers the following suggestions:

▸ Have an interesting and inexpensive extracurricular program.

▸ Arrange for schools to be open after school and in the evening for activities children can participate in.

▸   Establish clear guidelines that prohibit gang activity.

▸   Encourage responsible citizenship through teaching problem-solving and nonviolent dispute resolution (see "Conflict Resolution" on pages 35–36).

▸   Contact parents immediately if there are signs of gang involvement. These signs might include graffiti; handsigns; the wearing of certain colors, clothing, and jewelry; and drug and other criminal activity.

For more information about gangs and what schools and parents can do about gangs, contact the National School Safety Center (see page 22) or:

●   The National Criminal Justice Reference Service
    Juvenile Justice Clearinghouse
    P.O. Box 6000
    Rockville, MD 20850
    Toll-free telephone: 1-800-638-8736

SEVEN WAYS TO PROTECT YOUR CHILDREN FROM GANGS

1. Make sure that your children are supervised after school and engaged in meaningful activities.

2. Get to know your children's friends and their families, and make sure that you know exactly where your children are at all times, what they're doing, and who they're doing it with.

3. Hold school informational meetings for parents, teachers, and students about gang recruitment, identification, and activities.

4. Look for these signs in your children: grades slipping, going out without telling you where, being friendly with known gang members, carrying weapons.

5. Establish and enforce curfews for your children.

6. Ask schools to adopt district policies that protect children who are threatened and harassed by gangs. These policies should prohibit the wearing of gang symbols and colors. (See "Dressing for Safety" on pages 52–54.)

7. Ask the school to start gang awareness classes.

Bigotry and Ethnoviolence

Bigotry exists all over the world, so it comes as no surprise when its ugliness surfaces in schools. Bigotry often leads to violence, and some schools are even being closed because of it; in May 1993, South Boston High School was shut down for a week after a fight between white and black students. Whether dislike or hatred is based on race, ethnicity, national origin, religion, age, disability, gender, or sexual orientation, it all amounts to the same thing: ignorance.

Schools are an ideal place for children from all cultures to learn to understand and like each other and eliminate that ignorance. Schools can also be leaders in teaching the importance of understanding all sides of an issue before taking a position. This concept is important because bigotry thrives on accepting ideas without questioning or understanding. In working toward this goal, many schools are now instituting classes to teach students how to get along with one another. The classes include eliminating students' misunderstandings of and anger toward people who are different from themselves. The students talk about hateful words and other word associations, and about how jokes about race are not funny but hurtful. They talk about solving fights through mediation, not violence.

What can schools do to bring students closer together? Here are some ideas you might suggest to your child's school:

▸ Bring in a bias reduction program for both students and teachers. Just as parents and students can hold bigoted feelings (either conscious or unconscious), so can teachers and administrators. For more information and referrals to curricula, contact one or both of the organizations listed on page 50.

▸ If a national or local incident involving bigotry is featured in the news, have students talk about it in class.

▸ Get kids working together on projects like musical bands, sports, yearbook projects, clubs, and other activities.

▸ Insist that all graffiti is removed immediately. See Chapter Six, page 98.

▸ Develop a system for reporting all crimes and incidents, including hate crimes, to the principal and to law enforcement (see pages 39–41).

▸ Bring to the attention of the principal and the board of education any textbooks or other classroom materials that promote bigotry, directly or subtly.

▸ Encourage the use of textbooks and classroom materials that promote tolerance and understanding. An example: *Respecting Our Differences: A Guide to Getting Along in a Changing World* by Lynn Duvall (Free Spirit Publishing, 1994) encourages young people to become more tolerant and learn more about the people around them.

▸ Develop a school survey on race relations. Invite input on the questions from parents, students, and teachers. Initiating such a dialogue is a great way to start improving everyone's feelings and perceptions of one another. For help with forming survey questions, see the Spring 93 issue of *Teaching Tolerance* magazine or contact Teaching Tolerance directly; see below.

▸ Open a dialogue on "hate language." While our current sensitivity to remarks that can be construed as "hate language" is certainly going to lead to positive changes in the way people communicate with and about one another, we need to start differentiating between language that is merely offensive and language that is truly hate-filled or threatening. Otherwise we may become afraid to talk to one another at all.

To report hate crimes and/or to ask for advice and help on bigotry, call the Community Relations Service of the United States Justice Department toll-free at 1-800-347-HATE (1-800-347-4283).

For more information about bigotry and what schools, parents, and students can do about it, contact:

● Teaching Tolerance
  The Southern Poverty Law Center
  400 Washington Avenue
  Montgomery, AL 36104
  Telephone: (205) 264-0286

● The Anti-Defamation League
  B'nai Brith
  823 U.N. Plaza
  New York, NY 10017
  Telephone: (212) 983-5800

▼ ▼

SIX WAYS TO DISCOURAGE BIGOTRY IN YOUR CHILDREN

1. Take an honest look at your own attitudes toward people who are different from you. Make a real effort to educate yourself and become more accepting of others.

2. Realize that children who exhibit hateful and bigoted behavior have learned it from adults. Such behavior doesn't come naturally.

3. If other adults in your life make bigoted remarks in front of your children, tell them that their remarks are not okay with you. Don't tell bigoted jokes, and explain to your children why they shouldn't either.

4. Encourage your children to think about how other people feel. Teach them to be empathetic. Make sure they know that prejudice is unfair and they shouldn't exclude children from their group of friends for reasons of prejudice. Suggest that they tell students who say or do bigoted things that their words and actions aren't fair or right. Acknowledge that speaking up in this way takes courage, and show your support.

5. Talk with your children about how different physical attributes (hair, eyes, skin color, body types, disabilities) are not "strange" or "funny," just different. Don't make bigoted remarks about the way people look. If your children make such remarks, explain why they are wrong and hurtful.

6. Don't assume that all conflicts between people of different races involve racism. Some disagreements have nothing to do with the races of the people who are disagreeing, and they are more likely to be resolved if race isn't introduced as an issue.

▼ ▼

Dressing for Safety

If James wears a leather jacket to school or Irene wears a beautiful gold necklace, they both risk having these desirable, expensive items stolen from them. Or, as is increasingly common, if Bobby wears a certain team jacket that a gang has adopted as its theme, he may be subjected to violence by gang members. Equally as troubling, if Jennifer thinks that wearing a see-through blouse will make her sexy and popular, she's wrong; it may be seen by others an invitation to harassment or worse. Clearly, what students wear to school can have a significant effect on their safety.

Although there has been no official research yet on the impact of clothing on safety, nor any significant court cases, it makes sense to heed anecdotal reports in newspapers that kids are often the target of violence and crime due to what they wear. Happily, there is a lot parents can do to guide children to dress safely. Discuss the following "don'ts" with your children. Make sure they understand why they should think carefully about what they wear to school.

▸ Don't wear T-shirts with derogatory or offensive messages—profanity; sayings promoting drug use, violence, gangs, alcohol, or sex; messages promoting anything else that is illegal, immoral, or obscene; words, phrases, or pictures showing bias against others because of race, ethnicity, religion, gender, or sexual orientation. Shirts like these are just asking for trouble, and not only from other students. Students who wear them also risk offending staff and being treated with less respect.

▸ Don't wear expensive items like leather jackets, fur coats, watches, or whatever athletic shoes are most popular at the time.

▸ Don't wear gang colors and clothing. If there are gangs at your child's school, find out about their colors and clothing. Make sure your child doesn't wear anything that might be mistaken for gang involvement. Gang clothing often involves certain bandannas, caps, jackets, hairstyles, jewelry, shoes, and shoelaces.

▸ Don't wear revealing clothing—short shorts, pants that are very low-slung, see-through blouses, miniskirts, tight skirts, pants, or sweaters. These can invite harassment, abuse, even violence.

Some schools are instituting outright bans on these forms of clothing. Former New York City Schools Chancellor Joseph Fernandez notes that in New York "the central board sets minimal guidelines for dress for the thirty-two local boards in the five boroughs: no shorts or see-through blouses, no shoes with metal cleats that can damage furniture, no ornaments or symbols that might be inciteful (like a KKK badge or swastika), no radios, no beepers, no hats, and so forth. Some things you can't restrict, like length of hair. The courts found that to be an infringement on personal rights."[36] Many schools in California are also instituting bans; so is Detroit.

Opponents to school dress codes claim that these codes violate individual rights as guaranteed by the First Amendment. The American Civil Liberties Union (ACLU) offers to mediate for students who feel that their rights have been infringed by school dress codes. The ACLU has expressed concern about dress codes, fearing that they could potentially censor students' political opinions or send the message that any clothing fads, particularly those of black and Hispanic students, are gang-related.[37] However, most education and safety experts agree that dress codes work and are here to stay, and that schools have the right, even the responsibility, to uphold them.

Some schools go so far as to institute uniforms. As explained in an article in the *NASSP Bulletin*, "Uniforms can serve as a symbol or representation of the organization, certify the individual as a legitimate member of the organization, and conceal status. They can promote a feeling of oneness among students and can reduce the difference between the haves and the have-nots."[38]

It is generally agreed among experts that it makes a lot of sense for kids to be careful about what they wear to school. Whether you would like to see your child's school adopt dress codes or uniforms, or you just want to help your child avoid "dangerous" clothing, there is a lot you can do to help your child dress safely. Don't complain about strict codes; they are there to protect your child.

Talking with Children about Dressing for Safety

It's not just the ACLU that equates clothing with individual rights. Kids do, too. Don't be surprised if your children insist that they should be able to wear what they want, wherever they want, and that they aren't "afraid" of gangs.

You might use this as a lead-in to a discussion about individual rights and things that are and aren't worth fighting for. For example, you might agree that your child has a right to wear what he wants, then ask him if it's worth getting attacked or shot over. You might suggest other ways he can exercise his right without asking for trouble: "Instead of wearing your team jacket to the mall, you could wear something else you really like, then save your jacket for parties at your friends' houses. You'll still get to wear your jacket, just not to the mall."

Newspapers and news magazines often feature stories about students who tangle with school administrators about dress codes. Sometimes the parents respond by pulling the children out of school and suing the school. These stories are good discussion-starters, too. You might share them with your child, then ask questions like, "Is this issue really worth throwing a child's education into turmoil? Is it worth suing the school?" You might also consider the questions, "Whose fight is this really—the child's, or the parents'? What's the parents' agenda? Is it in the student's best interests to pursue this issue?"

The decision of what to wear to school is often influenced by peer pressure. When kids say, "But all of my friends are doing it," a normal parental response is, "If your friends jumped off a bridge, would you jump, too?" It's important to understand that the answer to that question, *from the child's perspective*, is, "Yes, I would." Your challenge becomes one of suggesting a "bridge" that's not quite so high or so dangerous. For example, your child might say, "All of my friends are wearing [a famous brand of athletic shoes], and I don't care if they're gang shoes—we like them and I'm going to buy some." You might respond, "Wearing those shoes could be dangerous for you and your friends. I notice that most of your friends are wearing [a famous brand of sweatshirt]. Those don't seem to be gang-related. How about if instead we buy you a sweatshirt in whatever color you choose?" In this way, you allow your child to save face and retain some control over her life and her decisions. She's happy, you're relieved, and the issue of what to wear to school has been resolved...at least for now.

3

Discipline

▼▼

A playground aide is afraid to report a child's unruliness because she fears that the school and/or the child's parents will overreact and punish him too hard, perhaps even beat him. A fight occurs at your child's school, and your son tells you that teachers just stood around watching the action and doing nothing. A girl steals a pencil from another student and is suspended from school for an entire month. A disruptive student is sent to a well-run classroom for the rest of the day, but he bothers students there, too.

These are obvious cases where school discipline was not effective and, in fact, jeopardized student safety. Matching consequences to students' negative actions is a challenge schools face every day, and parents know all too well how hard it is to do the same at home.

Schools *and* parents can make things easier by realizing that student disruption is caused by two factors:

1. Students carry a lot of "baggage" to school, including home-life problems and societal problems.

2. Schools don't always manage students effectively. Their discipline policies can contribute to or even provoke bad behavior.

For example, if a school or administrator uses inappropriate classroom or supervision practices, students will misbehave. On the other hand, if children are treated with dignity and respect, they will most likely respond with the same. As author and former school principal Barry Raebeck observes, "In my experience, discipline problems aren't the result of what kids do, they're the result of what adults do—or don't do. Indeed, too often a school's discipline's practices are based on erroneous assumptions about why kids act the way they do."[1]

If incidents are ignored, or if they are noted but no action is taken, then kids will act out more. When prompt and appropriate action is taken against infractions, more are reported although fewer actually occur. Some teachers are afraid to enforce disciplinary measures because they think they may be sued by parents or even dismissed by the district. However, experts in school safety say that courts usually uphold and support teachers' efforts to keep students under control.[2] Most parents want schools to be under control as well!

What Parents Can Do about Discipline

Most importantly, parents must realize that they *do* have responsibility for the way their children act in school. Likewise, schools must realize that the way they handle students makes a big difference in their behavior.

If there are discipline problems at your school, you might want to start a committee comprised of the principal, parents, teachers, students, and even local law enforcement officials to investigate what can be done. Look at two areas of discipline in particular: classroom control by the teachers, and when and why teachers turn students over to the principal for more severe discipline.

Ask the principal for a copy of the school policy on discipline. If there is no written policy, working with the administration to prepare one will be the first task of your committee. If the policy is insufficient, your committee can rewrite it. For help with this task, call the National School Safety Center (NSSC) at

(805) 373-9977 and request information on discipline. Principals' associations have literature available as well.

Your policy should make it clear which actions are affected. Parents and schools should know the difference between actions that need school disciplinary measures and actions that are criminal and need law enforcement involvement. The distinctions must be clearly stated in the policy.

School misconduct is behavior which is unacceptable to administrators but does not violate criminal statutes. Absenteeism, tardiness, disrespect, inappropriate language, smoking, cheating, and lying are some examples of misconduct. Examples of crimes needing police intervention are assault, vandalism, extortion, arson, and possession or use of alcohol, drugs, or weapons. For more on misconduct vs. crime, see "When Should Schools Call the Police?" on pages 40–41.

Your policy should clearly detail examples of actions to be taken, divided between the first occurrence and repeated occurrences. Each action can have a minimum and maximum consequence, which can range from an informal talk to parent involvement, to conference, to short suspension, to long suspension, and, finally, expulsion. Publicize the new policy and contract. Make sure that all parents and teachers are aware of it.

Take a look at detention. Is the time students spend there productive? It should be or it is a waste of time. Better to get at the cause of the problem with mediation and resolve the issue; see "Conflict Resolution" on pages 35–36.

If detention and suspension don't seem to be working in your school, you can form a group to establish an in-school alternative learning center. These centers are good solutions to discipline problems because they keep disruptive students in school while separating them from the other students. The staff of the center can take the time to help the students solve their problems. Like many major changes, schools sometimes feel that this one is expensive and difficult to implement, but schools that have alternative learning centers say that they solve problems rather than create them. Call the NSSC for a referral to resources that can help you set one up at your school.

If your own child consistently needs discipline at school, request psychological testing. Often this can be arranged through the school at no charge to parents. Psychological testing can help to identify some possible causes of a child's disruptive behavior. These might include:

▶ *Giftedness.* A gifted child who is not sufficiently challenged by school may get bored and restless.

▶ *Learning disabilities, or learning differences.* A child who can't keep up with the class or who feels left out or "dumb" can become a behavior problem.

▶ *Emotional problems.* These may require counseling or treatment.

Once you know the reason(s) behind your child's disruptive behavior, you can start working with the school on solutions, and your child can have a more positive school experience.

The publisher of *Safe at School* also publishes several books for and about children who are gifted and those who have learning differences. For more information and a free catalog, call Free Spirit Publishing toll-free at 1-800-735-7323.

How Should Teachers Respond to Student Fights?

There are several reasons why teachers and staff sometimes ignore fights and other disruptive behaviors, including:

▶ They may fear for their own safety.

▶ Breaking up fights is too much trouble.

▶ Breaking up fights is stressful, especially if staff are not skilled in doing so.

For schools to be safer places, all staff members must be well versed in effective ways to intervene in student disruptions that have the potential for becoming violent or have already become violent. These include knowing:

▶ what to do with bystanders

▶ what to say and what not to say

▶ how to find out what's really going on

▶ what to tell the students involved in the disruption to do

▶ how to report disruptions

▶ how to prevent similar occurrences from happening in the future.

If a student has a weapon, the first response should always be to isolate the student if possible and call the police immediately. Sometimes the best tactic is to tell the armed student to leave the building. Call the NSSC for referrals to programs that train teachers how to break up fights.

As a parent, you need to tell your children this vital message: *"If someone has a knife or a gun, do not try to disarm the person. Get away and tell an adult."*

Corporal Punishment

Corporal punishment means that teachers and principals may use "reasonable force" to restrain students and "maintain the order necessary to conduct an educational program."[3] In most states that allow corporal punishment, "reasonable force" means more than just grabbing or pulling a student. It means that the student can be beaten, paddled, hit, or spanked, even if parents have specifically requested that their child not receive corporal punishment. Most psychologists, pediatricians, and other health professionals feel that corporal punishment should be abolished.

While schools must have a way to protect themselves against knife- and gun-carrying hoodlums, "using force for self-protection is not considered corporal punishment," as the National PTA points out.[4] A look at the 1993 *Deskbook Encyclopedia of American School Law* shows that out of ten lawsuits filed against schools for beatings, at least seven were filed on behalf of young children who were not committing crimes or violent acts.[5] These students, ranging from kindergartners to sixth graders, had received corporal punishment for "offenses" including talking, laughing, hitting another student after being kicked by that student, and fooling around in gym class.

According to the National Coalition to Abolish Corporal Punishment in Schools, the United States is one of the very few countries that still permit corporal punishment.[6] Japan, Israel, the United Kingdom, China, and Russia do not allow educators to hit children. We still have 26 states that allow it. Of these, the following ten states have the highest percentage of students paddled each year: Arkansas, Mississippi, Tennessee, Alabama, Texas, Oklahoma, Georgia, Florida, Louisiana, and Kentucky. In the states that allow corporal punishment, many cities have individually abolished it, including Atlanta, Houston, Miami, and Seattle; Washington, D.C. has also abolished corporal punishment. More than 40 major organizations favor abolition of corporal punishment, including the American Academy of Pediatrics, the American Medical Association, the American Psychological Association, the National Committee for Citizens in Education, the National Education Association, and the National PTA.

The National Coalition to Abolish Corporal Punishment in Schools presents these and other compelling arguments against corporal punishment:[7]

1. *It perpetuates a cycle of child abuse.* It teaches children that it is acceptable to hit someone smaller and weaker when angry.

2. *Children are injured, sometimes severely.* Injuries from corporal punishment have included cuts, bruises, and broken bones. Some children in the United States have died from injuries received during school corporal punishment.

3. *Certain groups and types of students are punished more often than others.* Children most likely to receive corporal punishment include poor children, members of minority groups, children with disabilities, and boys.

4. *Schools are the only institutions in America in which striking another person is legally sanctioned.* Corporal punishment is not allowed in prisons, in the military, or in mental hospitals.

5. *Corporal punishment can lead to lawsuits.* Educators and school boards are sometimes sued when corporal punishment is used in their schools.

The best argument against corporal punishment is this: Many alternatives are available that have been proved to work better. These include "emphasizing positive behaviors of students, realistic rules consistently enforced, instruction that reaches all students, conferences with students for planning acceptable behavior, use of staff such as school psychologist and counselors, detentions, in-school suspension, and Saturday schools."[8]

▼ ▼

SIX STEPS TOWARD ELIMINATING CORPORAL PUNISHMENT

If corporal punishment is still practiced in your child's school and you would like to try to get it banned, follow these suggestions from the National Coalition to Abolish Corporal Punishment in Schools:[9]

1. Talk to friends and other parents about corporal punishment. Share with them the information in this chapter and ask if they will join you in your efforts to ban corporal punishment.

2. Contact the National Coalition for materials. See below for the address and telephone number. Be sure to request their videotape, "Changing School Board Policy: Corporal Punishment."

3. Obtain from your local school board a copy of your district's policy on corporal punishment. This policy should spell out how, when, and by whom corporal punishment can be used. Ask your school board how many times corporal punishment was used in the past school year. They should be able to give you this number.

4. Organize a meeting for parents, teachers, and community members. Invite members of organizations that favor abolition of corporal punishment (see page 59).

5. At the meeting, read aloud the local policy and review materials from the Coalition. Open up discussion about concerns and show the video. According to Coalition director Nadine Block, "One of the most important benefits from viewing this videotape is it allows parents to examine their own child rearing practices without feeling they're being scrutinized or preached to by people outside the family."[10]

6. If the superintendent does not support changing the policy, contact the Coalition for additional information on how to build a larger effort. Write or call:

● National Coalition to Abolish Corporal Punishment in Schools
155 West Main Street, Suite 100-B
Columbus, OH 43215
Telephone: (614) 221-8829

The National PTA also has a booklet about corporal punishment called "Discipline: A Parent's Guide" that you may find useful. Write or call (and be sure to request their catalog):

● National PTA
Publications Orders Department
700 North Rush Street
Chicago, IL 60611-2571
Telephone: (312) 787-0977

▼ ▼

4

Arrivals and Departures

▼ ▼

Angela wants to know why her family car has safety belts but her school bus doesn't. Matthew, a fourth-grader, insists that he is old enough to walk to school with his friend, even though he has to cross a busy street. Dale's parents want their baby-sitter to be the driver in a carpool, but they are not sure if this is a good idea. And Rosa, who rides her bike to school, resists wearing her helmet.

The parents of these children, like parents everywhere, need to find ways to get their children to school and back home safely. Whether the trip is a brief ten minutes or an exhausting hour, school commuting time is fraught with questions and anxieties about dangerous situations that our children are likely to encounter without our protection. Fortunately, there are ways to educate ourselves, our schools, and our children to prevent problems.

School Bus Safety

Angela is not alone in wondering why her school bus doesn't have safety belts. For years, parents have voiced their concerns about lack of belts to school boards, school bus manufacturers, and the National Coalition for School Bus Safety. With the help of this parent pressure and new safety studies, child safety advocates in New Jersey (including New Jersey PTA lobbyist Phyllis Scheps) finally won the first state law requiring seatbelts in new school buses; it took effect in 1992. Says Arthur Yeager, D.M.D., national coordinator of the National Coalition for School Bus Safety, "Kids know you don't ride in vehicles unless you have a restraint."[1] And parents and school bus drivers know that belts keep children seated, orderly, and safe and prevent them from putting their heads and arms out the window.

Other cities and individual communities have installed seatbelts in their buses even without a law requiring them. But what if your child's school bus is one that still does not have safety belts? If it has the newer, padded, higher seats, the child's body is protected by "compartmentalization," according to the National Safety Council. But optimum protection comes from seats *and* belts, so you might wish to call the school board to state your views, tell your school safety committee to pressure the administration, and call your state legislators to request a law similar to New Jersey's. Be sure to ask that the law include wording requiring that the belts be worn. Some states and cities where buses are equipped with belts do not require that students actually use them.

School bus monitors improve safety, too. Monitors are adults who are paid to ride the bus and help children board and exit safely. Although they can be expensive, monitors have been found to be especially helpful on buses where the students are in grades K through 3. Children of this age have been run over and even killed while passing through the "death zone," a ten-foot area around buses where drivers cannot see.

Monitors help keep kids orderly *inside* the bus as well. Nancy Bauder, president of the National Coalition for School Bus Safety, understands how hard it is for drivers to supervise kids and drive at the same time. "How many teachers turn their backs on a class of 60 to 90 children for two hours a day?" she asks.[2]

Another new development in school bus safety is the use of video cameras to monitor children's behavior. Districts that use these install a black box with a blinking red light in every bus in a fleet. They purchase only a few cameras, however, since it would be too costly to buy one for every bus. The cameras are rotated regularly, in secret, and since it's impossible to tell whether the camera is in the box, everyone must assume that today is the day their bus has the camera. Even the drivers don't know.

These surveillance devices are a very effective way to cut down on undisciplined behavior, especially in older children. Crime, bullying, harassment, and smoking are caught on tape, as are fights, verbal rudeness, and vandalism. The tapes can be used as proof to suspend bus privileges for disruptive students. Due to their success in improving safety, video cameras on school buses are becoming more popular and prevalent.

What You Can Do about School Bus Safety

According to the National Coalition for School Bus Safety:

▸ Over 9,500 injuries and 10 fatalities occur per year inside school buses.

▸ 500 injuries and 40 fatalities occur outside buses (in the "death zone").

▸ An estimated 50 additional fatalities occur inside buses on field trips.

▸ 12% of the 350,000 school buses in the United States date from before 1977, when new safety rules took effect regarding fuel tanks and flammable seat materials.

Working through the school safety committee or your parent safety group, request these improvements to the buses in your district:

1. Seatbelts.

2. Bus monitors.

3. Video surveillance.

4. Extra-wide convex mirrors and "STOP" arms with flashing lights to improve "death zone" safety.

5. Roof hatches for better exiting if the bus rolls over (it does in 11 percent of all school bus accidents).

6. Two-way radios for emergency communication with headquarters.

7. An object detection system that senses motion in blind spots. It attaches to the front bumper and stops the bus automatically if anything touches it.

8. Loudspeakers for drivers to direct students.

9. Ask to have bus roofs painted white to reflect the sun's heat, cooling the interior of the bus and producing better behavior.

Make sure that your child knows the bus safety rules. You'll find a list on page 67 of this book. You may want to make a copy and post it on the refrigerator or family bulletin board for easy reference. Kids need constant reminders!

If you *really* want to get involved in school bus safety, try one or more of these:

1. *Call your state department of transportation and ask for a copy of your state's school bus safety standards.* Compare these to what your district is doing.

2. *Take a ride on a school bus.* Look at things from a child safety point of view.

3. *Ask your school if it provides regular school bus safety instruction and evacuation drills.*

4. *Complain strongly if students must stand because there aren't enough seats.* If the buses are equipped with seatbelts, insist on rules about using them.

5. *Ask about inspection and maintenance routines for buses.*

6. *Check out your child's bus route.* If you've got an idea for a safer route, ask the board of education to reroute the bus.

7. *Alert local police if you notice that citizens in cars are passing stopped school buses.*

8. *Ask the board of education about driver screening and training requirements.* Don't forget substitute drivers, who often are used for field trips.

According to the 1993 *Deskbook Encyclopedia of American School Law,* "Courts have often found school bus operators negligent and their employers liable for injuries received by passengers when the injuries are the result of a failure by the operator to follow generally accepted standards of good judgment in the operation of the vehicle."[3]

Demand that drivers be hired *after* the district has received their prior driving records, not before. It's very hard for districts to find good drivers because of the unusual hours required by the job, so watch for shortcuts.

9. *Ask about the age of the buses in your district.* School buses should be no older than 10 to 13 years. Call your state department of education for information on your state's specific laws.

10. *If your child will be attending a preschool program by bus, or if your child is physically challenged, call your district's transportation office to discuss safety plans.*

BUS SAFETY RULES

1

Get to the bus stop just on time. Too early, and waiting creates risk. Too late, and running causes falls. Stand on the sidewalk while waiting.

2

Always cross the street in front of the bus, not behind it. Wait until the bus has stopped, the safety lights are flashing, AND the driver sees you and says it's okay to cross.

3

Stay out of the "death zone," the 10-foot area around the bus.

4

Never stop on your way toward the bus or go back to pick up something you dropped. Alert the driver or another adult.

5

Carry all supplies in a book bag, not in your hands. Don't block aisles with belongings.

6

Sit in your seat quietly. Buckle your seatbelt if available.

7

Never put any part of your body out of the window. Children have been killed this way!

8

Don't distract the driver. Don't yell, throw things, or misbehave.
Keep your hands to yourself.

9

Stay alert. Don't doze.

10

Get to know the driver. Be nice to him or her. (This goes for parents, too.)

Walking to School

Matthew, the boy who wants to walk to school, is flexing his independence muscles, which is terrific. But the busy street he has to cross is only one of many factors his parents must consider before they decide he is ready to walk to school with a friend. Another is his level of maturity and that of his walking companion. When they are together, do they fool around, or can they be trusted to "do the right thing"?

If Matthew's parents feel that the boys can be trusted, they next need to determine whether the children are able to read traffic signs and understand how they actually relate to traffic. For example, if Matthew and his friend know that a red light means "stop," do they also know the "right-turn-on-red rule" (if it applies to their state)? If they know the rule, do they also know how it affects intersection traffic? According to child safety experts, this "cognitive" awareness only comes when a child is between ages 9 and 12. Although many children younger than this are allowed to walk to school, their parents are probably overestimating their ability to handle traffic and other street safety situations.

According to the National Safety Council, these are the ways in which 70% of all pedestrian accidents occur:[4]

1. *Darting out.* A pedestrian enters the street mid-block and is hit by a moving vehicle.

2. *Walking along the roadway.* A pedestrian is struck while walking on the edge of the road.

3. *Ice-cream vending truck.* A pedestrian is hit while walking away from the truck after making a purchase.

4. *Vehicle backing up.*

5. *Multiple threat.* A pedestrian is hit while crossing a multi-lane street.

6. *Vehicle turning or merging.*

7. *Intersection dash.* A pedestrian is hit while walking in a crosswalk or crossing the street with the light.

8. *Bus stop.* A pedestrian is hit by the bus.

Matthew's parents then need to give him a serious lesson in crossing the street. If possible, they should take both Matthew and his friend out for a practice session.

▼ ▼

HOW TO CROSS THE STREET:
SIX STEPS TO PRACTICE WITH YOUR CHILDREN

1.   Look for a corner or crosswalk at which to cross. Plan a route that includes crossing guards.

2.   Stop your feet at the curb.

3.   Look for any traffic signals.

4.   Listen for sirens or horns.

5.   Look both ways, then cross.

6.   Walk quickly. Don't run. Watch for traffic.

   TIP: Exaggerating the how-to steps—big gestures, wide-open eyes for "looking"—will maximize understanding.

▼ ▼

Dangerous People

   Children who walk to school must also know what to do if they encounter problems from people on the street. Strangers, thieves, bullies, molesters, drug dealers, and gang members all are real dangers for children on the way to school. In many urban areas, this is perceived as a bigger problem than traffic. The situation can get so severe that children are too afraid of street activity to go to school.

   If fear is interfering with your children's ability to walk to school, it's time to take strong action.

▶   Start by talking to them to determine the source of their fear. Listen carefully and don't dismiss or belittle anything they say. Their fears are real to them, even if they seem trivial or silly to you.

▶   Walk the route with them several times. Often this can eliminate or lessen children's fears. Point out safe places they can run to if they have a problem—"block parent" houses (see #5, page 70), police stations, post offices, banks, and other businesses. Workers with uniforms are another option. Make an effort to get to know neighbors and businesses along the way so your children will feel comfortable approaching them.

Review the following guidelines with your children and make sure they know and understand them. In relatively safe areas, this additional personal preparation may be enough to reduce your children's fears—and yours.

1. *Always walk with at least one other person.*

2. *Know your address, phone number, and parents' work numbers.* Know how to make phone calls from public telephones.

3. *Carry identification at all times.*

4. *Don't carry valuables that can be visible targets for thieves.*

5. *Know which houses belong to "block parents."* These houses display signs indicating that a child in trouble can ring the doorbell for help.

6. *Don't wander off by yourself.* Avoid lonely places.

7. *Don't accept rides from anyone unless your parents have made arrangements ahead of time for you to ride with that person.*

8. *Never go anywhere with anyone who doesn't know a family code word.* Parents, it's smart to establish a "code word" in the event of an emergency. For example, if you are injured and must send someone else to pick up your children from school, that person should know the code word.

9. *Yell or scream "FIRE!" if someone tries to make you do something you don't want to do.*

10. *Give muggers anything they want.* Don't resist. Try to stay calm. Try to remember a description of your attacker. Get away as soon as you can and report the attack to the police, your school, or your parents.

11. *Know who is a stranger and who isn't.* Parents, discuss this in detail with your children. Even someone they have seen before—like a neighbor—is a stranger if you don't know the person's name and your families aren't acquainted.

12. *Ignore strangers who try to start conversations with you.* Don't answer questions. If possible, move away by crossing the street.

13. *Don't "help" strangers.* Adults don't need children to help them.

14. *Listen carefully when your parents tell you about "stranger danger," but remember that all strangers aren't bad.*

15. *Don't carry any weapons.* They will more likely be used against you if you try to use them.

In high-crime areas, you'll need a combination of personal preparation and community support. Work with your community law enforcement agencies to help make streets safer, especially during before- and after-school hours when children need to get to school and home.

One idea suggested by the National School Safety Center is the Safe Corridor concept.[5] Police organize to block off and guard major routes to and from the school during critical hours, such as between 8 and 9 a.m. and again between 3 and 4 p.m. They make their presence well-known, and as long as kids can get to these major routes, they'll be safe.

Almost all communities now offer some kind of crime watch and/or drug watch program with citizen participation. Look into how these can make school commuting safer in your city or town.

▼ ▼

ARE CHILD IDENTIFICATION SYSTEMS USEFUL?

Some schools and communities have instituted "child identification systems," such as fingerprinting children. While these might seem on the surface like good ideas, they are no substitute for adequate supervision and training. In fact, the National PTA has come out strongly *against* child identification systems. Delegates to the 1987 National PTA convention passed a strongly worded resolution that reads, in part:[6]

"WHEREAS, Misinformation and noninformation abound in child identification programs because they too often focus on stranger abduction and exploitation; and

"WHEREAS, Parents need to be aware that acquaintances, not strangers, commit most abductions and sex crimes against children; and

"WHEREAS, Schools need to be aware that a thumbprint is useless to law enforcement in locating missing children and that only a complete set of ten fingerprints on an official FBI card will assist in the recovery of a missing child, as recommended in the 1983 National PTA resolution, 'Child Fingerprinting Identification;' and

"WHEREAS, Most commercial child identification systems fail to include court records and custody orders which are necessary for prompt recovery in family abduction cases;...therefore be it

"Resolved, That the National PTA encourage local PTAs to contact the National Center for Missing and Exploited Children for technical assistance and review of materials which may be exploiting the issue of missing children."

The only "child identification system" I recommend is a picture ID card similar to an adult's driver's license. These cards are sometimes referred to as "student IDs" and are available through government service centers. Or you might suggest that your school provide picture IDs for students.

▼ ▼

Kidnapping

More kids are kidnapped by noncustodial parents than by strangers. The National Center for Missing and Exploited Children warns of the possibility that children of divorced parents will be abducted from school by the noncustodial parents.[7] Often, commuting time is used to kidnap the children.

To make sure that a noncustodial parent doesn't pick up your children from school, give the school certified copies of your custody decree to keep on file. Ask to be alerted immediately if the noncustodial parent makes unscheduled visits to the school or requests to leave the grounds with your child. Tell the school about any threats made to snatch the child.

Carpooling

Dale's parents want to carpool, which is an excellent way to save time, money, gas, and stress. However, if their baby-sitter is going to participate, they should let the other families know ahead of time, in case someone would prefer that only the parents drive.

If your baby-sitter drives the carpool in your car, she is covered under your insurance policy. If she (or he) uses her own car to drive your children and others, you must check on her coverage. Chances are that a young or low-paid baby-sitter will have only minimum coverage. You should also check on whether your insurance covers your child riding in her car.

Take carpooling seriously, as it's a huge responsibility. For example, if children from other families are injured in your car, there is the possibility that the parents will sue you for payment of medical bills. In addition, there are laws requiring you to have a commercial auto license if you accept money over and above compensation for gas mileage.

Should teenagers drive to school? That depends. Driving to school isn't a "right," as many teens seem to feel. It's a privilege. Some schools are beginning to restrict who is allowed to drive to school, both for safety and for academic reasons. Check with the school before letting your teen be part of a carpool. Even if the school gives permission, go one step further: Take a ride with the teenage driver and check the safety of his or her driving.

▼ ▼

FIVE RULES OF SAFE AND HAPPY CARPOOLING

1. There must be enough seatbelts for each child (no sharing) and they must all be buckled up. Every state in the U.S. now has laws requiring children to buckle up. Belts must be worn even if there is an air bag on the front seat passenger side.

2. All participants must agree that the driver may tell all children what to do. In other words, if a child is misbehaving, the driver can insist on good behavior.

3. Continually late or disruptive members will not be permitted to stay in the carpool.

4. If a driver is substituted, all members must be alerted.

5. Pick-up and drop-off procedures must be safe and legal. Principals around the country are alarmed at the number of carpools that don't follow school's lane rules and wait for students in fire lanes or bus lanes. When in doubt, ask the principal where carpools should deliver and wait for riders.

▼ ▼

Biking to School

Rosa balks at wearing her helmet when riding her bike to school; she claims that helmets are "hot, heavy, and funny-looking." Actually, she's right. But they do their job—saving lives. Because they work so well, communities are passing laws *requiring* children to wear helmets. Currently New Jersey is the only state to mandate helmets for bike riders under age 14. Since the law was passed in 1992, helmet use has risen from 3% to 40%, and bike fatalities have been reduced by half.[8]

When the law was first passed, there were lots of letters to the editor in New Jersey newspapers both for and against requiring the use of helmets. The letters against helmets said the government too often tells people what to do. The letters for helmets were from grieving parents whose children had been killed or seriously injured when helmets could have saved them. The latter, often filled with graphic details, were far more compelling.

Don't wait for a law to be passed in your state requiring children to wear helmets. Insist that bikes and helmets are inseparable—for riding to and from school and at all other times. Here's why:[9]

▶ Over 350,000 children under age 15 are treated in emergency rooms yearly from bike accidents.

▶ Nearly 50,000 suffer serious head injuries.

▶ Around 400 die each year from bike accidents.

▶ Helmets reduce the risk of injury by 85%.

Before you let your child ride his or her bike to school, review the bike safety rules on page 75. Make sure your child knows, understands, and agrees to follow these rules. You may want to make a copy and post it on the refrigerator or family bulletin board.

▾ ▾

BIKE SAFETY RULES

1

Wearing a helmet is mandatory and not negotiable.

2

Before you leave for school, think about what you need to carry. Is the weather likely to change between morning and afternoon? Will you need warmer clothes? Is there a safe place to store the things you will be carrying? A heavy backpack can make it harder to ride and keep you off-balance. A front basket or rear-wheel packs are safer and easier to use.

3

Know, understand, and obey all traffic safety rules.

4

If the law in your town or city allows it, ride on sidewalks instead of streets.

5

Keep your bike in good working order.

6

Make sure that your bike is the right size for you. Bikes that are too big are not safe. Your feet must be able to touch the ground when you are sitting on the bike seat. Lower the seat if necessary—or ride a smaller bike.

7

Walk, don't ride, your bike through intersections.

8

Get a copy of the bike safety manual published by your state motor vehicle department. Read it and study it.

9

Protect your bike from theft by:
▸ registering it with the police
▸ buying the best lock and locking chain you can afford
▸ using the school bike rack.
Hiding your bike in the bushes makes it easier for thieves to break the lock and steal your bike without being seen.

▾ ▾

Street Safety around the School

"We need more crossing guards."

"Why isn't there a crosswalk on that side of the school?"

"What are they waiting for, someone to be killed?"

You might have heard other parents make comments like these about street safety around your school. You might have made these comments yourself. You are wise to be concerned.

Parents expect the streets around schools to be safe, and they have a right to expect them to be. They also have the right to ask local traffic safety officials to look at and remedy unsafe situations. But things are not as simple as that.

For example, parents often are dismayed when their requests for traffic signals and crosswalks are denied. But often a traffic signal would not really have solved the problem. For example, to avoid the new light, many drivers might take back roads and make turns they ordinarily would not have made. This may force more cars and traffic down other roads near the school. Even if efforts to get a new traffic signal are rewarded, it might take forever for the light to be installed, due to red tape.

Don't let the drawbacks stop you from trying to win traffic safety improvements. Start by finding out which government level has responsibility for the street in question: town, city, county, or state. If the principal doesn't know, call your local traffic safety professional (municipal engineer, town supervisor, mayor, councilperson, police) and ask who's responsible. Call or write about the problem.

Easy requests include fixing potholes in front of the school or cutting back overgrown shrubbery that interferes with visibility. You will be told to call the appropriate maintenance crew. If the problem plants are on private property, authorities will usually write a letter to the owner, requesting that the shrubs be cut back within a specified period of time.

Perhaps you have noticed that there needs to be a stop sign posted at an unsigned corner near your school. Maybe the sign is broken. Or you think a yield sign should be replaced by a stop sign. All of these situations are usually more involved, and local authorities need to do extensive evaluations before arriving at a decision to grant or deny a request.

The hardest street safety improvements to win are often the most desirable. These include:

▶ passing an ordinance to restrict unsafe parking situations.

These kinds of laws are often requested by either parents or residents on streets near schools. Sometimes it's the residents that request the ordinance, claiming that when parents park to pick up their children, it creates safety problems. Sometimes it's the parents who request it, claiming that other parents are parking in ways that are dangerous to child pedestrians.

Other hard-to-win improvements are:

▶ lowering speed limits around schools

▶ adding crosswalks and crossing guards

▶ installing a traffic signal.

Traffic signals are the most frequently requested improvements and the hardest to achieve. They are also the most frequently misunderstood. There is a long list of requirements that must be met before a traffic signal can be installed, mainly because they are very expensive to install and maintain—from $120,000 to $250,000 and up. Fortunately, school crossings are often given priority for new traffic signals. But approval depends on factors like:

▶ minimum vehicle volumes

▶ interruption of continuous flow of traffic

▶ minimum pedestrian volumes

▶ number and type of accidents

▶ hourly traffic volumes

▶ peak rush hour delay times.

If conversations with authorities do not produce any action at all (not even a meeting to discuss the problem), consider drafting a petition and getting parents at your school to sign it. Contact local businesses to get the chamber of commerce involved. Call the local media and give them the story. Almost everyone in a community has a stake in wanting safer streets.

Safety Patrols

If being the member of a "safety patrol" at your school involves helping other children to cross the street, setting up traffic cones, or directing cars or buses, you might want to think twice about letting your child participate. Some schools assign these tasks to upper elementary grades even though many state laws prohibit children from directing traffic. The New Jersey school board association laws clearly state that the board is not liable for injuries a child may incur as a member of a safety patrol.

If safety patrol members work inside the school—for example, leading younger children to recess—that is acceptable. However, I strongly recommend that patrols *not* be used for street crossings. We have all read stories about heroic kids who have pulled younger children out of the paths of oncoming cars. In fact, children should not be risking their lives for other children! When schools need someone to guide children across busy streets—and most schools do—they should use adult crossing guards. In my opinion, there is no alternative.

Before- and After-School Care at School

Whether your child now spends her afternoons after school at home, at grandma's, at a child care center, in family day care, in a latchkey situation, or at a baby-sitter's, very soon she may be spending her after-school time at...school! It has always seemed natural that school buildings be used for more than the hours between 8 a.m. and 3 p.m., when traditional classes run. But it has taken a long time for any major changes to be made in their use, for several reasons: Who would be in charge of before- and after-school programs? Who would pay for them? Who would supervise them?

More people have been searching for answers to these questions because more parents than ever require before- and after-school care for their children. Innovative solutions abound in schools around the United States. Some programs are run by the schools themselves, some by parent groups, some by township recreation departments, and others by the YMCA and other community groups.

Children's advocates know that these programs are much needed, but they also know that they need to be monitored. Due to the innovative nature of many programs, there has arisen a need to standardize this kind of care.

The National Association of Elementary School Principals (NAESP), together with the Wellesley College School-Age Child Care Project, has written *Standards for Quality School-Age Child Care,* which establishes 19 "standards of excellence" that provide safe and secure after-school environments for children ages 5 to 13. You might also be interested in a booklet from the NAESP called "The Right Place at the Right Time: A Parent's Guide to Before and After School Child Care." Both can be ordered from:

- NAESP Educational Products
  1615 Duke Street
  Alexandria, VA 22314-3483
  Telephone: (703) 684-3345

At the time of this writing, the price of *Standards for Quality School-Age Child Care* is $19.95; "The Right Place at the Right Time" is $3.00.

These publications cover topics ranging from how to find schools with after-school care to what you should look for in a program and what parents' responsibilities are. They also cover safety and health considerations. Since school-run programs may not have to be licensed by the state, *Standards for Quality School-Age Child Care* advises parents to make sure that any program they are considering for their child meets or exceeds what would be the expected standards for licensed programs. Also to look for: check-in and checkout procedures, the staff-to-child ratio, and the physical space size for the number of children involved. In addition, who are the staff? They should at least have undergone standard background checks. (For more on background checks, see "Teacher, Administrator, and Staff Crime" on pages 183–186.)

Especially important are the program's plans for older children (ages 10 to 13) who can easily become bored in a program set up for younger children. Boredom leads to problems.

Starting a Program: What You Can Do

If you want to look into starting before- and/or after-school child care in your school, begin as always by contacting the parent organization first, then the principal. "Principals are sometimes not very excited initially by the idea of child care after school," says June Million, spokesperson for the NAESP. "They think it's one more thing for them to do, and they think, reasonably, that they already have enough to do. But in schools that have these programs in place, principals often find they solve problems rather than create more of them."[10]

You might want to survey the other parents to see how many of them want and need the program. On the survey, ask:

▸ whether parents want before-school programs, after-school programs, or both

▸ how many children in their family would be participating

▸ how many days a week the children would be using the program(s), and

▸ how much they would be willing to pay.

Also ask which parents might be needing the program in the near future, even if they don't need it right away.

Once you have the completed surveys, tabulate the results. With these figures in hand, provided there has been a large enough response to warrant starting one or more programs, you should be able to get a sponsor easily. A sponsor can be any organization that is interested in running the program, from your local YMCA to a town recreation department, the board of education, or a private child care company. Usually, sponsors manage programs as for-profit enterprises, with fees reflecting a combination of what community members can afford and what the sponsor needs to make the program financially feasible. Your parent group might want to do some "comparison shopping" to find the most economical option.

5

Supervision

▾ ▾

A teacher took students onto the roof of a school for a photography lesson. A girl stepped on a skylight, fell through, and died. In another case, a teacher was absent from her classroom during a fire drill and someone in the class was injured.

Are these teachers guilty of negligent supervision? These cases, reported in *Legal Notes for Education*, are still being decided.[1] They demonstrate the unfortunate fact that we parents can't always take it for granted that our children are being adequately supervised at school.

The amount and type of supervision in schools is almost always a very subjective decision. It depends on many variables, like the age of the children, the type of activity they are involved in, the physical space they are occupying, the available teachers, and the opinion of those in charge. There is not much factual information available about what constitutes proper supervision. I have come to the conclusion that this is probably because if schools established hard-and-fast rules about how many teachers should watch how many children and in what way, then they would have to follow these guidelines *always*, which would be impossible. If they had rules about supervision and failed to follow the procedures they established, they would be held liable for any injuries to students that occur. Therefore, what is proper only comes to light in the courts, where parents take cases that they believe are examples of negligence.

A survey of 500 school districts by the University of Kansas found that of 1,047 lawsuits filed against school districts by students, an overwhelming 821 were for negligence.[2] According to Michael Imber, professor of educational administration at the University, "Schools used to justify a large degree of control, but don't do so now; the 'in loco parentis' doctrine is not being used very much by the courts."[3] This means that schools used to be held much more accountable for the supervision of students than they are today. Schools are not necessarily liable if a child is injured when no teacher is present. It depends on why the teacher wasn't present. Did she stand for an hour chatting with a colleague, or did she have a good reason to leave the room for a brief period?

Parents, Schools, and the Law, published by the National Committee for Citizens in Education, reports that a teacher is not expected to anticipate every situation where one child may suddenly injure another. However, in a case where students were left unsupervised at recess and told to play baseball, boys throwing pebbles at a girl injured her eye. The school was found liable because if a teacher had been there, the teacher would have certainly stopped the rock throwing, which had gone on for some time before the girl got hurt.[4]

Supervision liability also depends on whether the school has had prior experience with a problem. If they know that a particular bathroom is the scene of much trouble and they fail to supervise it properly, a child who is injured there has a right to sue.

The bottom line on supervision is that it is a nebulous situation. Schools are not legally bound to provide a certain amount of supervision for any particular activity; the circumstances of each individual situation prevail. So what can parents do? Here are two suggestions to start with:

1. *Make sure that you know when supervision starts.* Ask the school specifically at what time in the morning it begins accepting responsibility for students.

Michael Imber advises parents to discourage kids from arriving at school too early, when there is no supervision. He says schools feel that parents have taken advantage of the fact that hanging around outside school is better than staying at home alone. If school starts at 8:30 a.m. but your child arrives at school at 7 a.m. because you must be at work, you might want to get together with other parents to hire extra supervision. At other schools, fee-charging before-school child care programs have solved this problem.

2. *Make sure that you know when supervision ends.* Again, ask the school. This time could be different for different children, depending on what grades they are in and whether they are involved in after-school activities.

Recess

Because so many children get hurt at recess, parents often want to know why there has to be recess at all, especially in light of the need for more time to fit in all of the regular curriculum. But recess has value in giving kids a chance to release some of the energy that builds up after being confined to their seats all day. Also, as noted in an article in *Principal* magazine, "In most elementary schools, recess is the only time when children are permitted to interact with peers of their own choice. Talking in the classroom is usually considered inappropriate behavior."[5] But what if recess is a problem at your school because of lack of supervision, injuries, fighting, or bullying? Here are some ideas to consider and try:

1. *Talk to your children about what happens at recess.* Try to get specific details. Are they unhappy at recess? Why? Do they often try to stay inside during recess? What are the reasons?

2. *If possible, visit the school during recess to see for yourself what is happening on the playground.* What do the aides do? When kids start playing too rough, do the aides intervene quickly? Do the children seem bored? Bored kids are more likely to start trouble. Do the aides interact with individual children or small groups, or do they try to survey the entire yard at the same time?

3. *Discuss the situation with the people who monitor recess.* They might have some good ideas. Ask for the possibility of more structured activity like games, or ask for equipment to be provided like balls or jump ropes.

4. *Talk to the principal about alternatives to traditional unstructured recess time.* Unstructured time often leads to trouble. Some schools offer aerobics in the gym or library reading time, for example.

5. *Look into the dynamics of "site supervision."* Can the recess supervisors truly see everywhere they need to? Where is the best place for the supervisor to stand to see as much as possible? In some cases, trees or shrubs may need to be cut back so kids can't hide out of sight and get into trouble.

According to Annie Barclay, president of the Educational Support Employees Association, "Recess aides should, at the minimum, have CPR and first aid training. Knowledge of behavioral intervention techniques is important, too."[6]

Schools that experience a lot of recess problems are starting to equip their recess supervisors with communications devices, such as walkie-talkies, so they can summon help quickly if the need arises.

Bullying

Speaking of recess problems, recess seems to be the time when children complain most about being bullied by other children. What does bullying involve? A bully is a child (or group of children) who extorts lunch money from another, threatens other children with violence, violates other children's civil rights, or picks fights with others. Bullying is more than roughhousing, says George Butterfield of the National School Safety Center (NSSC). "Bullying is a euphemism for criminal acts—crimes committed by young people that adults would be arrested for," he explains.[7] An NSSC report on bullying claims that "bullying is perhaps the most underrated problem in schools today."[8]

In the past, schools have looked the other way when it came to bullying. But the subject of how much responsibility schools should bear on bullying is changing. Bullying is starting to be recognized for what it is—a form of harassment that includes verbal and emotional abuse and physical attacks. With the proliferation of weapons in schools, the need to do something about bullying has taken on added urgency. George Butterfield thinks that parents should start to demand that schools provide a system for reporting and dealing with bullying. No child should ever have to put up with what bullies dish out.

The National School Safety Center offers these 3 "R's" of bullying prevention:[9]

▶   *Rules.* Parents and educators must demonstrate that they are in charge and won't tolerate any student hurting another student, physically or psychologically.

▶ *Rights.* Every student has the right not to be hurt and the right to learn in a safe environment.

▶ *Responsibilities.* Educators must be responsible for better supervision and more active and observant monitoring of the schoolyard. Also, students must be responsible for respecting the rights of their classmates and themselves.

In a conference about bullies with authorities from around the world, the NSSC came to these five conclusions about bullying:

1. School bullying is a significant and pervasive problem.

2. Fear and suffering are becoming a way of life for victims of bullying (and can even drive some to attempt or commit suicide).[10]

3. Young bullies are more likely to become criminals as adults and to suffer from family and professional problems.

4. The prevailing attitude that kids fighting each other are just experiencing normal youthful aggressive behavior must be discarded.

5. The United States should follow the lead of Scandinavia and Japan, whose governments have addressed bullying problems with national intervention and prevention programs.

▼ ▼

SIX THINGS YOU CAN DO ABOUT BULLYING

1. **Be alert to the signs of trouble.** Suspect bullying if your child is afraid to go to school or shows a lack of interest in school.

2. **Help your children learn to socialize well with peers.** They will be less likely to be targets of bullying. Manage their social life so they have frequent opportunities to make friends and be part of a group. Invite other children to your home often and encourage your children to form relationships with nice kids.

3. **If the bullying is ongoing, tell the school.** Ask school officials to take a student survey to find out the extent of the problem.

4. **Keep a written record of all bullying incidents, including names, times, dates, and circumstances.** Submit this report to the principal.

5. Never tell your children to hit back when they are threatened. Parents commonly tell their children to "fight back," but this often makes things worse instead of better. Saying "Leave me alone!" and then walking away is the best approach.

6. If you suspect your child is bullying someone else, consider family counseling to determine the cause of the problem.

See "Conflict Resolution" on pages 35–36 for information about a problem-solving technique that can also be used to address bullying. For more information about bullying, contact the National School Safety Center; see page 22.

▼ ▼

Verbal Abuse by Teachers

Has your child been ridiculed in front of the class by a teacher (perhaps about grades), been called names by a teacher, or been the target of vulgar language or of "fighting words" (aggressive words) spoken by a teacher? Then your child may have been the victim of verbal abuse.

If you believe this may have happened, here's one way to approach the problem:

1. First, *talk to your child about it.* Talk in depth over a period of time—days or weeks. Encourage your child to be as specific as possible and to remember all related information. No matter what the outcome is, help your child understand that talking to you about this is the right thing to do, and that learning to come up with a solution and implement it is a good life experience.

2. *Talk to other parents.* Have their children had any problems with this particular teacher?

3. *Talk to the teacher yourself.* Try to go in with an open mind. Be willing to hear the teacher's side. Express your confidence that this problem can be overcome. If you don't put the teacher on the defensive, you're more likely to win his or her cooperation and arrive at a solution.

4. *If you aren't happy with the results of the teacher conference, talk to the principal.* You may find that the situation can be laid to rest with a few apologies and

mediation by the principal between you and the teacher. In some cases, action needs to be taken against the teacher by the school or by the parents—perhaps disciplinary action or even dismissal.

Bathroom Issues

Sometimes children are made to feel embarrassed by the teacher for having to go to the bathroom during a crucial teaching lesson or other such time. While children *should* be *encouraged* to use the bathroom during recess and lunch, they should also be allowed to go at other times, especially if they are elementary school age. Doctors recommend that children under age eight should have unquestioned access to the bathroom but should also be carefully monitored.

Consider doing a "bathroom check" of your child's school. Make sure that the bathrooms are equipped with toilet paper, soap, and locks on the stalls. Often, schools don't fill soap dispensers in the students' bathrooms because the custodian doesn't want to clean up soapy messes. Since soap is necessary for proper hygiene, try to get this practice changed if it's a problem in your school. In addition, schools often take the locks off of bathroom doors because troublemakers go around locking all the doors and then climb out underneath. However, removing the locks penalizes the privacy rights of the many due to the misbehavior of a very few. Request that locks be reinstalled on bathroom doors to give children privacy and dignity.

Finally, school bathrooms should be monitored so bullies can't harass children who are using them.

Safety on Class Field Trips

You may be surprised to learn that class field trips are quite controversial and are often debated in academic circles and journals. An article titled "Are Most Field Trips a Waste of Time?" featured the opinions of two educators.[11]

Dr. Manu Patel of T.C. Williams High School in Alexandria, Virginia, wrote that field trips *are* a waste of time. Many students view them more as an opportunity to get away from classes than as a way to learn, he claims. (Try to plan a trip on a weekend, he suggests, and see how many students show up.) He also maintains that too many hours of preparation are required by the teacher for a truly effective trip—hours that include visiting the site beforehand, arranging transportation, and locating parent chaperones. He's concerned about students who can't see what's going on once they are there and will wander off. He's awed by the liability of the teacher for transportation safety.

Art teacher Janice Plank wrote that field trips *are not* a waste of time. She feels that they provide students with experiences that can't be duplicated in the classroom and help involve parents and the community in schools.

In many schools, the subject of whether field trips are worthwhile is moot, since budget cuts have eliminated most if not all trips from the curriculum. Those schools that don't have the money for trips are actually better off from the standpoint of safety. Why? Take a look at some of these real newspaper headlines:

▸ From the *New York Times:* "School Copes with Shock After Crash." The article tells of two children who died and 27 teachers and students who were injured when their bus went off the road on the way back from a class trip to Montreal.[12]

▸ Also from the *Times:* "On School Trips, Contracts Allow Searches for Alcohol." The article tells how teachers are allowed to search students for alcohol before they are permitted to go on trips. The need to conduct searches like these speaks volumes about student attitudes toward trips, which supports Dr. Patel's view that students look at trips as "fun."[13]

▸ From the Newark *Star-Ledger*: "Crime Mars Atlantic Students' Smithsonian Trip." Two eighth grade students from Atlantic County, New Jersey, were robbed by youths armed with a knife and a gun while on a class trip at the Smithsonian Institution's Museum of American History in Washington, D.C.[14]

▸ A story that received national attention: "Michigan Parents Worry Over Children on Snowy Outing." Over 100 students from a school in Bloomfield Hills, Michigan, were stranded by a blizzard while camping in the Great Smoky Mountains National Park in Tennessee.[15]

▸ From the *Times*: "Car Plows Into Children in Tour, Killing One." As the entire third grade from a school in Sycamore, Illinois, was touring O'Hare International Airport, a car went out of control and plunged into them on a walkway. One child was killed and dozens were injured.[16]

▶ And this case reported in *Parents, Schools, and the Law:* A 12-year-old boy on a field trip to a museum was beaten up by non-school boys. This occurred when teachers told students to break up into groups to look at the exhibits. Even though most parents would find this a serious breach of supervision, the school was found not liable because museums are not inherently dangerous places.[17]

Of course, there is always the argument that many more trips succeed without incident. While this is true, it's probably just as true that field trips are not the best use of scarce funds and time, especially in light of the legal liability that schools face should an accident occur. While all schools ask parents to sign waivers before the trip, these may not hold up in the event of a serious problem.

What if your child's class plans a field trip? Here are specific steps you can take to make the experience safe for everyone.

▶ Review the school bus safety rules with your child, especially if your child doesn't normally ride the bus to school. See page 67.

▶ Also review the rules about general street and stranger safety. See pages 69–71.

▶ Remind your child that the trip is for learning, not for playing around.

▶ If at all possible, volunteer to go on the trip. Schools always need parent chaperones for field trips. Also, this gives you an opportunity to see what really happens on class field trips.

Another way to get involved is to find out how class trips are planned. In many cases, the teachers individually plan the trips; in other cases, a school-wide committee plans all or some of them. Ask if you can sit in on the planning process, or form a parent committee to participate.

One suggestion that represents a good compromise: Instead of long-distance trips, make more use of nearby community resources such as banks, supermarkets, businesses, post offices, fire stations, etc. Too often, trips to these community gold mines are relegated to nursery schools and kindergartens. In fact, older children are more likely to be interested in them and to benefit from an understanding of how they function.

Of course, you always have the option of not permitting your children to go on a scheduled field trip, although this is the least preferable solution. Schools sometimes offer parents the choice of having their child sit in on another classroom during an all-day field trip. But children who can't go on trips feel left out and might even suffer repercussions from the teacher. (For example, what if there is a follow-up quiz on the field trip?)

It's amazing how many schools plan trips that many, if not most, parents would rather their children not go on. My daughter's class went on a field trip in her second week of kindergarten. She was having enough of a problem adjusting to school when suddenly she was taken two hours away to an apple orchard and returned at 4:30 p.m after another two-hour bus ride. The parents who went on the trip said that it was exhausting, many children cried, and it was simply not worth it.

The very best solution in terms of safety, money, and time is to bring the world to the school instead of sending the children on trips. There are many educational programs available that can come to schools and bring their world with them, including art shows, animal presentations, science demonstrations, and cultural performances. As museums and theaters feel the financial crunch of reduced visits by schools, more and more of them are providing these kinds of services.

Overcrowding

What constitutes an overcrowded school? A school district that has 2,000 more students enrolled than it can accommodate. A kindergarten class with 70 children sharing desks. Schools where classes are held in basement storage rooms because all the regular classrooms are being used. These are just some of the true examples of overcrowded conditions in schools around the United States.

Overcrowded schools not only make learning much more difficult, they are also extremely unsafe. Too many children squeezed into schools creates tension and stress which leads to disruptive behavior. The National School Safety Center advises that "student populations in excess of 1,100–1,200 students are much more difficult to supervise."[18] Too many children supervised by too few teachers can lead to acting out and injuries. Put too many children into a school, and the principal can't know everyone by name, so kids can't feel special. This leads to alienation and isolation.

How do schools get overcrowded? One way is simply that more families with children move into an area than the local schools were built to accommodate. Another way is that the building of additional schools has been postponed because of lack of funding. Another way is that teachers are laid off or not replaced, again because of funding shortages, and classes become too large as a result.

Closely related to overcrowding are large schools that are *meant* to house thousands of students. In larger-than-normal schools, students feel the same stress and alienation experienced by those in too-crowded schools. Children feel totally cut off in large schools. They are treated like numbers. If they are upset or having problems, it is much less likely that someone will notice and help them in a large school than in a smaller one.

Sometimes all it takes to remedy overcrowding is convincing a district to hire another teacher to split a class of, say, 46 into two classes of 23. Other times, students can be bused to nearby schools. But most of the time, there isn't anything much that parents can do besides apply continual pressure to build a new school. Relief from overcrowding usually has to come from very high up. However, you might try asking the district to "reevaluate enrollment capacity" at your school. This kind of study can get things started and lead to changes.

What should you tell your children to do to stay safe if they are attending an overcrowded school? Explain that everyone else has to deal with the same situation and the same frustrating feelings. Explain that just because someone has bumped into them isn't a reason to get angry; if halls are too crowded, these things happen. Reinforce the strategies for avoiding fights discussed on pages 43–46.

Crowd Control at School Special Events

In December 1991, eight young people were trampled and crushed to death and 29 others were injured at the entrance to a gym at City College. They were waiting to enter the gym to watch a charity basketball game featuring celebrity rock stars. Somehow, a stampede started—the *New York Times* called it a "deadly human wave"—and the people at the front of the line were pressed against a locked door at the bottom of a stairwell. They had no way out.

Although this situation happened at a college, it could easily happen anywhere, at any school. The management of crowds is a fine art that is often left to inexperienced people, as was the case at City College, and is the case at many school-sponsored events.

Schools host many wonderful activities such as carnivals, festivals, concerts, dances, ceremonies, and sports events. Sometimes the events are coordinated by school administrators, sometimes by community groups, and sometimes by parents. For example, parents who want to do fundraising for all the great safety improvements mentioned in this book may one day find themselves in charge of managing hundreds or thousands of people in the course of achieving that goal.

Following are some essential strategies and steps related to crowd control, as suggested by experts in event management and the National School Safety Center. They are important for you to know if you are involved with planning large events, and also if you and your children are attending events where there are large numbers of people.

▼ ▼

CROWD CONTROL: WHAT YOU CAN DO

▸ If you're in charge, consult with school administrators and security personnel at every step of the way. Communicate clearly and carefully.

▸ Even if you feel uncomfortable making suggestions about safety that might intrude on the festivities, stand firm.

▸ Start planning far in advance of the date. Think through and write down every step of the event, including which people will be where and when.

▸ Look for places where students might climb to get a better view of the event, and therefore get hurt—like trees, ledges, portable toilets, bleachers, etc. Plan to block them off (or, in the case of portable toilets, locate them away from trees, fences, etc. that people can climb to reach the top).

▸ Plan to close off sections where you don't want people to go. Use signs, security guards, yellow police tape, or portable fencing.

▸ If food will be served, don't sell anything in bottles or cans; they can be broken or thrown. Use paper cups only.

- ▸ Prohibit pets from all events.

- ▸ Form a customized evacuation plan in case of emergency.

- ▸ Be aware that the longer the event, the more time there is for problems to occur, so keep it short.

- ▸ Send your written plan to local law enforcement officials, fire marshals, etc. and ask for their input and suggestions. Revise your plan accordingly.

For outdoor events:

- ▸ Have a plan B for adverse weather conditions.

- ▸ Make sure ample water is available and easily accessible. This is especially important for hot days.

For indoor events:

- ▸ Look for ways to increase ventilation.

- ▸ Do not hold indoor events without controlled tickets. Sell (or, for free events, distribute) the same number of tickets as you have seats available.

- ▸ Do not allow or attend events with "festival seating," where people are permitted to stand in a given space. Festival seating can lead to deaths and injuries from people pushing and crowding to get in front. In 1992, the National PTA created a formal resolution opposing festival seating.

▼ ▼

Special Planning for Sports Events and Potentially Violent Crowds

Most violence and trouble at school-sponsored events happens at sports events—football, basketball, and hockey games and other competitions where tension and rivalry run high. The National School Safety Center offers lots of advice about keeping sports events safe. Here are some excellent suggestions from the NSSC and other experts:[19]

▶   If there is intense rivalry between competing teams, choose a more neutral site, and/or designate separate entrances and restrooms for each team.

▶   If there is a great deal of tension between the schools, don't hesitate to postpone games.

▶   Try to schedule games to be held during the day rather than at night.

▶   Enlist aid from community agencies. For example, ask a marked patrol car to sit at the entrance, and ask police to drive by during the event.

▶   Offer free admission to police officers and their families and the faculties of both schools to increase visible authority. (Many communities find that asking as many dads as possible to attend events increases security and cuts down on problems.)

▶   Specifically prohibit alcohol, drugs, and weapons, and warn spectators in advance if pre-entry searches are planned.

▶   Post school rules and read them over the public address system.

▶   Require student ID's.

▶   Have bullhorns available to address the crowd. Give security personnel two-way radios or walkie-talkies.

▶   Make sure that parking and walking areas are well-lit.

▶   In especially violent areas, plan "bullet drills" where students are told in the event of gunfire to lie face down until the "all clear" signal is given. Better yet, consider blocking off nearby streets to avoid drive-by shootings.

Finally: If you are attending a school event and trouble starts, don't stay around to see what happens. Leave the area as quickly as possible. Instruct your children that they are to do the same in your absence.

For more information about planning for special events, contact the NSSC; see page 22.

"It isn't enough to worry about grades if the schools are falling apart."

ELLEN GOODMAN[1]

6

The Building and the Playground

▼ ▼

John is disgusted with his son's school: the bathrooms are without toilet paper or locks on the doors, the roof leaks, and windows are constantly broken. Eileen wants to know if there is anything she can do to help the school fight the graffiti that mysteriously shows up overnight. Maria is concerned because her son is being asked to do work in the school that she thinks is the job of the custodian.

These parents have children who are attending schools where the lack of proper maintenance is causing health and safety problems, and they want to know what they can do about it. There is actually a *lot* that parents can do about these matters. But first, let's understand a little about school maintenance.

School Maintenance

Underfunded and/or poorly managed maintenance is one of the most visible safety issues in schools. In some cases, this is because the schools are just too old to be functioning well. Many schools, especially those in big cities, were built before World War II and some were even built before the turn of the century. A survey by the American Association of School Administrators, reported in *Schoolhouse in the Red: A Guidebook for Cutting Our Losses*, reveals that:[2]

▸   30% of school buildings now in use were built before 1950

▸   21% in the 1950s

▸   22% in the 1960s

▸   14% in the 1970s

▸   11% in the 1980s.

The study reports that the older buildings are not passing safety regulations, and debate over whether to close them or renovate them can drag on for a long time. In many cases, it costs more to renovate than to build new schools. The study also reports that many of the schools built in the 1960s were built too fast, used low-quality materials, and have huge energy inefficiencies.

Another reason why older schools are a problem to renovate is because of the lack of utilities. Science labs and shop classes need running water and gas lines that may be impossible to install safely. New computers require heavy-duty electric lines and surge protection that can't be economically inserted into older buildings. Even basic electrical safety is a problem for some schools. Many newer state electrical codes require ground fault interrupters to prevent accidental electrocutions, but most schools were built before these codes went into effect. Since schools are "grandfathered"—exempt from conforming to new laws because of previously existing conditions—they are not required to install the interrupters. Funding them may be a good project for your parent committee.

According to *Wolves at the Schoolhouse Door*, a study from the Education Writers Association:[3]

▸   61% of the nation's school buildings need immediate repairs

▸   42% pose environmental hazards

▸ 33% are only adequate, and because of growing enrollments and deferred maintenance could easily become inadequate

▸ 25% are in shoddy condition

▸ 25% are overcrowded

▸ 13% are unsound structures.

In his book, *Savage Inequalities: Children in America's Schools*, Jonathan Kozol describes schools that had to be closed twice in one year because the toilets overflowed; in another school, dust from crumbling plaster turned kids' hair white.[4] *NEA Today*, a publication of the National Education Association, reported that many school boilers are just waiting to explode because no one is trained to work on them.[5] The *New York Times* reported that in New York City, "The Board of Education has permitted its school custodians to operate under so few controls that they have managed second careers on school time, fabricated ghost employees on their payrolls and hired helpers with criminal records."[6] A management consultant examining mismanagement in Newark schools found 3,400 backlogged repair requests for 1988; by 1993, that number had grown to 6,000, with 1,300 more requests coming in monthly.[7] Clearly school maintenance is a serious problem, and if schools and school districts aren't doing enough about it, then parents must take action.

The Custodian

Who is supervising our schools' custodians? In many districts, custodians do not report to the principal, but instead to someone at the board of education. This can make it hard for the principal to direct what goes on in his or her building. On the other hand, many principals aren't eager to take on this authority because "with meager funds for repairs and supplies, they know *they* will be blamed, instead of the custodians, for filthy or hazardous conditions."[8]

While there is not much parents can do about custodial supervision, they can do things like insist on soap and toilet paper in the bathrooms (and fund these if necessary). Some parents have even contracted with nearby buildings like YMCAs to have their children use their bathrooms when the school's are unusable or too horrid.

Another way for parents to influence school safety concerning custodians is to bring the following list to the attention of their principal. (Never interrupt a custodian directly with any requests.) These criteria were suggested by George Butterfield of the National School Safety Center.[9]

A good custodian:

▶ congenially confronts unknown people encountered in the building

▶ feels a sense of ownership of the school campus

▶ locks workrooms while not using them so children can't get into them to steal or hide (workrooms have also been the scenes of rapes and assaults)

▶ has a lock and unlock schedule for every door on campus

▶ considers every door and when and why it needs to be locked, then unlocks only according to need, at exact times and for specific reasons

▶ keeps a clean school and therefore a safer school

▶ targets graffiti for immediate attention, even before kids get to school.

Graffiti makes schools look sad and neglected, so it must be removed immediately. (If the graffiti is a bias saying, take a photograph and call in local law enforcement before destroying it.) Parents might want to band together to purchase a pressure washer so the custodian can blast graffiti off of school property quickly and easily. There is also a new type of paint being developed that won't let graffiti stick.

▾ ▾

TAKE A SAFETY WALK

The safety committee at your school should conduct twice yearly safety walks to examine the school for maintenance and other safety problems. *This is one of the most effective ways for parents to see, report on, and influence safety in their schools.*

Here's what to do:

1. Take a preliminary walk. Meet with the principal and possibly the custodian as well and explain that you will be walking around the school grounds and interior looking for safety hazards. The principal may want to tell you of specific sites that he or she knows need attention. You can all walk together, but don't let the principal guide you away from any area you wish to see.

2. Take detailed notes of everything you have questions or concerns about.

3. Ask the principal to invite the assistant superintendent or other head of maintenance from the board of education in your town to come to the school to discuss what you have noted. You should attend this meeting as well. Ask what capital improvements the town is planning for your school; also ask if there has been a recent survey of structural deficiencies.

4. Plan together the repairs that should and can be accomplished. Set a timetable.

5. Schedule another walk at the end of the school year to monitor what has been done and what still needs doing.

What should you look for on your safety walk(s)? *Schoolhouse in the Red* contains a "School Facility Evaluation" checklist that explains what parents and other concerned persons can look for in the following areas: school walls, ceilings, floors, structural supports, doors, painting, electrical systems, lighting, heating, cooling, ventilation, food service, plumbing, restrooms, grounds, playgrounds, athletic fields, handicapped access, enrollment square footage, energy efficiency, environmental problems, and general maintenance and operation. To obtain a copy of this report (at this writing, the cost is $6.95), write or call:

- American Association of School Administrators
  1801 North Moore Street
  Arlington, VA 22209
  Telephone: (703) 875-0748

▼ ▼

Children as "Custodians"

Children are being hurt and worse when doing jobs in schools that properly belong to custodians. Kids have been killed while moving top-heavy TV carts; even when the equipment was secured, the carts have toppled over on them. Often these duties are assigned as school "safety patrol" or "service squad" activities, purporting to foster "responsibility" but really making things more expedient for school staff.

According to an article published in *Gifted Children Monthly*, the smartest kids are being asked to do these dangerous jobs because they can be "trusted."[10] In fact, in most schools any child might be asked to do these things.

Tell your children that if school employees ask them to help with custodial services, they should refer all such requests to you (as in, "You'll have to ask my mom/dad if it's okay"). Then state politely but firmly that you would prefer your children *not* perform such duties while at school. Tell your children that they should never move (or help to move) audiovisual equipment, cafeteria tables and chairs, pianos, gym equipment, or other large objects. You might want to write a note to the principal explaining that you don't want your children involved in these activities.

Some people maintain that while "helping the custodian" is clearly not appropriate for elementary school students, it might be okay for high school students under certain circumstances. I would discourage it for *all* students for safety reasons.

Playground Safety

Most of us have fond memories of fun times at school playgrounds when we were children. I remember a carousel that seemed to spin faster than our Buick, a slide that was as tall as the pine tree that grew next to it, and swings with horse heads that provided an equestrian thrill I never experienced in real life.

The playground equipment I recall with such affection is now known to cause most of the over 200,000 playground injuries children suffer each year, according to the National Safety Council. "Too fast," "too tall," and "too obstructive" are the words used to describe much of the equipment we enjoyed. Falls onto ground that's "too hard" account for 70% of these injuries and even cause deaths.

To address this problem, in 1991 the United States Consumer Product Safety Commission (USCPSC) published a *Handbook for Public Playground Safety* that outlines in detail several guidelines for public playground equipment safety. To date, manufacturers of playground equipment are trying to comply with as many of these guidelines as they can, but not all of them in equal amounts. California has turned these guidelines into law, and other states are considering doing the same. Call or write your state legislators to urge your state to adopt them into law. For a free copy of the handbook, write to:

- Consumer Product Safety Commission
  Washington, DC 20207

A minor caution: Although the information contained in the handbook is excellent and comprehensive, the technical language may be difficult for the lay person to understand. You may need to ask an expert for help in translating some of the terms.

Another issue affecting playgrounds is the Americans with Disabilities Act (ADA) of 1992. This federal law mandates that at least 25% of play events at public playgrounds must be accessible to individuals who are physically and mentally challenged. Since the law has not specified exactly how this is to be accomplished, confusion reigns as to the best way to proceed. One issue of special concern is the best way for wheelchair occupants to access equipment. Current thinking favors transfer stations—platforms that enable children using wheelchairs to move from the wheelchair onto the equipment—as ramps have not only proved too costly in terms of money and space, but also have the problem of being attractive to bike riders, roller skaters, and skateboard riders.

Guidelines for Safe Playgrounds

Getting hurt on a school playground, whether it's a skinned knee from falling onto asphalt or a broken arm from falling off a slide, is viewed by most parents and school workers as a childhood rite of passage. This has probably come about because in the past, playgrounds were not really designed with safety in mind. One has to wonder how anyone could have installed an eight-foot-tall slide over blacktop and called this a good place for children to play.

The USCPSC *Handbook* recommends specific safety standards for public playgrounds. These are outlined below. Compare them with the playgrounds at your school. If the equipment at your school was installed before 1991, it will probably not conform to these standards. Since most equipment currently in use predates 1991, it's clear that parents and communities have a lot to do to make playgrounds safer for children.

1. *Surfacing*. The material that covers the ground under playground equipment is by far the most important factor in preventing injuries. As noted in the USCPSC *Handbook:* "Because head impact injuries from a fall have the potential for being life-threatening, the more shock-absorbing a surface can be made, the more likelihood that the severity of injury will be reduced. However, it should be recognized that all injuries due to falls cannot be prevented no matter what playground surfacing material is used."[11]

Acceptable surfaces under equipment are:

▶ special rubber mats placed over asphalt, or

▶ loose-fill materials like wood mulch, wood chips, sand, or fine gravel.

The depth of the loose-fill materials required depends on the "critical height" of the equipment it is under. The *Handbook* specifies the maximum acceptable height for all kinds of equipment.

Unacceptable surfaces under equipment are:

▶ asphalt or concrete

▶ dirt and grass.

Their shock-absorbing properties are not sufficient.

High-level discussions are currently underway as to which surfaces meet the requirements of the Americans with Disabilities Act (ADA). Apparently, some guidelines from the *Handbook* conflict with accessibility standards for individuals who are physically and mentally challenged. The most likely outcome is that certain wood-mulch preparations will be found to meet both USCPSC standards for shock absorbency and ADA requirements for wheelchair accessibility.[12]

Another surfacing problem identified in the *Handbook:* "Tripping hazards" including rocks, roots, and railroad ties.

2. *Layout.* How playground equipment is laid out and arranged contributes to how safe it is. For example, swings need a large amount of space around them, and slides must exit away from other playground equipment. These and other layout-retailed details are found in the *Handbook.*

3. *Equipment.* Playground equipment should not have sharp points, corners, or edges. It should be splinter-free. Protrusions or projections are dangerous for obvious reasons and also because children's clothing can get caught on them, which has been known to cause strangulation. (TIP: Scarves and drawstrings from jackets are especially dangerous; they can become stuck in equipment and strangle a child. Instruct your children to take off scarves before playing on equipment. Cut off drawstrings so they don't dangle.)

▶ Equipment should not have head entrapments, which are defined as openings of more than 3.5 inches and less than 9 inches.

▶ Climbing equipment should not be higher than 7 feet tall, with an 8-foot fall zone around it.

▶ Swings should have seats made of lightweight, impact-absorbing rubber. They should not be higher than 12 feet tall, with a 6-foot fall zone.

▶ Slides should be no taller than 7 feet, with a 10-foot fall zone.

Equipment considered too hazardous for public playgrounds includes animal swings, multiple-occupancy swings, swinging exercise rings, ropes, merry-go-rounds, seesaws, and trampolines.

What You Can Do about Playground Equipment Problems

Knowing all of the information in the *Handbook* and all of the laws regarding playgrounds is not enough to prevent injuries to our children. *We parents must do something about the existing problems.*

Schools are generally very receptive to parents getting involved in playgrounds, more so than other issues. Perhaps it's because school playgrounds have traditionally been equal parts community resource and school property. Perhaps it's because fixing them is so expensive that schools will take all the help they can get. I suspect it also has something to do with their high visibility. Most parents at one time or another have seen the playgrounds at their children's schools. Poor playgrounds are much more visible than poor reading scores. This may be one reason why playground improvements have long been a popular "cause" for parent groups.

There are two ways to effect playground solutions: acting on the problems that cost little to correct, and forming a committee to fund major improvements including new equipment.

EASY, LOW-COST SOLUTIONS

1. *Remove equipment that the CPSC deems inappropriate, or equipment that is badly damaged, rusted, or unstable.* The removal is done by district workers, so no one has to be paid anything. Don't give the used equipment to anyone else (individual or organization); it must be disposed of.

2. *Contact the manufacturer(s) of existing equipment to repair any damages and, where possible, to lower pieces that are too high.*

3. *Lock the gates or add police surveillance at night and on weekends to prevent vandalism.*

4. *Ask for a school staff member to be appointed to make daily rounds of the playground.* This person (most often a custodian) should check the area for broken glass from smashed bottles and other debris. He or she should also check the equipment for safety problems—sharp edges, loose bolts, cracked plastic and wood, rust, etc.. Manufacturers provide maintenance information for playground equipment, but if the equipment is very old, this information will not help much, especially if the equipment hasn't been maintained all along.

MAJOR IMPROVEMENTS

The second way to solve playground problems—forming a committee and purchasing new equipment—may sound daunting, but it's doable (although it is a lot of work). We did it at my children's school and so have other parent groups across the United States. Follow these steps:

1. *Talk to other parents to find out their level of interest in forming a playground committee.* Introduce the idea at a PTO or PTA meeting.

2. *Get permission to proceed from (in this order) the principal, the school board, and the town.*

3. *Once approved, appoint a chairperson or even two co-chairs.* (We had co-chairs; this works well because there is so much to do.) Appoint at least three or four committee members and assign these tasks to them:

   a. Contact residents with expertise they can lend. Examples: physical education experts, child development experts, recreation directors.

   b. Prepare a questionnaire to distribute to parents. Ask what they would like to see in the playground. Beware: many will ask for equipment which has been judged taboo by the CPSC. You can explain why in a later memo.

   c. Make a list of old and new playgrounds nearby to visit, then visit them. Take pictures, make reports on the pros and cons you see, watch children play on them (including your own), and make note of the manufacturers of the equipment. (Most attach identifying plaques somewhere on the equipment.)

   d. Write for your free copy of the *Handbook for Public Playground Safety*. See page 100.

e.   Contact the manufacturers whose names you gathered on your playground tours and request copies of their catalogs. Call the toll-free operator at 1-800-555-1212, give the manufacturers' names, and see if they have toll-free numbers (most do). Or call the National Recreation and Parks Association at (703) 820-4940 for a free list of manufacturers complete with addresses and telephone numbers.

4.   *Set a tentative date for completion of your playground.* This may see several revisions.

5.   *Arrange a regular schedule of meeting times and places, either weekly or every other week, that is convenient for key committee members.* This may be the most difficult part of your project!

6.   *Determine the ages and numbers of children who will be using the playground.*

7.   *Decide where your playground will be located.* Like the completion date, this decision may see several revisions, although there usually is one site that is a clear favorite.

a.   Think about whether to keep or change the location of an existing playground.

b.   Look at shady vs. sunny times and places.

c.   Contact neighboring property owners to counteract any "NIMBY" problems (Not In My Back Yard.) Most neighbors will see nearby school playgrounds as an asset, but you've got to know what they're thinking ahead of time to avoid problems later.

d.   Identify any water drainage problems and soil condition problems. Initially, these problems can be identified by groundskeeping personnel and playground equipment representatives. They must be corrected by the town before equipment is installed.

e.   Make sure there is enough parking available (or space for parking), there are no dangerous traffic spots right near your site, and the site is accessible by wheelchair, as required by the ADA. For example, the playground can't be located up or down a flight of stairs or at the bottom of a steep cliff, unless you plan on installing an elevator to the site.

f.   Think about security. Don't put the playground in a remote, hard-to-supervise place.

8. *Get ready to do some serious fundraising.* Money doesn't grow on monkeybars, and playgrounds cost anywhere from $10,000 to $100,000 or more, depending on the size and equipment.

   a. Talk to the board of education to see if they will allocate funds from the town for all or part of your playground. You may hear, "But if we give to you, we'll have to give to everyone." Come up with rebuttals ahead of time as to why *you* need the money *now.* The most effective way to do this is by presenting your research on safety problems at your school playground, combined with the information from the CPSC.

   b. Ask the board and superintendent how to apply for any grants you may be entitled to. Grants are sometimes available from the state Department of Natural Resources, Department of Education, and Department of Conservation. There are Life Safety Code grants, Economic Incentives grants, ADA funds, and others.

   c. Ask local businesses and nearby corporations for donations.

   d. Plan fundraising activities to be conducted by your parent organizations. Suggestions: auctions, tee-shirt sales (the tees can have a playground theme), craft sales, used book sales, carnivals, hobby hours, bake sales, penny drives, and buy-a-playground-part drives.

   e. Create and post signs to let the community know about your project and your fundraising activities.

9. *Study the manufacturers' catalogs you have received.* Besides the equipment, look at warranties, specifications, pricing, and size of each company you are considering. Find out how long each company has been in business, check references, and contact local Better Business Bureaus. Compare companies.

10. *Decide whether to purchase wood or metal components.* Although many people find wood more attractive, metal is becoming more popular because it lasts longer. All wood used in playground equipment is treated with a compound containing arsenic to preserve it. Also, wood "checks" (cracks) after a period of time.

11. *Choose your components and colors.* You'll have a lot to choose from: panels, double slides, curly slides, tunnels, roller slides, fire poles, ribbon slides, wave slides, horizontal ladders, ring bridges, loop arches, clatterbridges, suspension bridges, arch bridges, corkscrew climbers, and more. You'll also want to include

some free-standing components: sandboxes, talk tubes, spring riders, balance beams, funnel balls, slides, swings, fitness stations, tetherballs, basketball hoops, benches, tables, bike racks. Consult with your town's disabilities coordinator for input on equipment for physically and mentally challenged children.

IMPORTANT: *Never buy equipment meant for residential use.* You'll save money initially, but the equipment will not last nearly as long and may not meet safety standards for public playgrounds.

12. *Choose your favorite three manufacturers.* Ask for a list of their clients and visit their playgrounds, if possible. Invite manufacturers' representatives from the three companies to visit your school and give presentations.

   a. Find out who designs the playgrounds—the salesperson or a design professional. In our experience, a design professional was preferable. Salespeople don't always have the necessary expertise, although they are often given the responsibility.

   b. Don't let the salespeople cloud your judgment. They are all pleasant and persuasive, and some are high pressure. Grill them with questions about warranties, insurance, and pricing.

   c. Ask for discounts; you'll get them.

   d. Negotiate shipping and installation costs. These will be much higher than you anticipated!

   e. Request written proposals from each company and compare them point-by-point.

13. *Decide whether to install your playground all at once or over a period of one, two, or three years.* Installation over time is called "phased installation."

14. *Decide whether you want the manufacturer to install the equipment, or whether your group wants to hire a supervisor to oversee and certify parent installation.* Professional installation costs from 20% to 60% of the price of the equipment, but this, too, is negotiable. Professional installation seems to be the safe way to go, although to save money, many parent groups go the supervisor route. In either case, make sure the installers check the location of underground lines—gas, electric, phone—before starting to dig.

   Good luck!

Safety During School Renovations

Thousands of older schools will be undergoing renovations in the next decade, so it is very likely that at some time your child will attend a school where renovation is going on. In best-case scenarios, much of the work will be started the minute school lets out for the summer and be completed before school opens again in the fall. Often, however, renovation work will be in process while children are in school, mostly because such a large amount of work can't be completed in just the summer months. However, certain jobs—like asbestos removal, floor refinishing, and roof work—should not be done during school hours due to the large amount of dust and fumes. Other jobs, like painting, can usually be managed when children are on the premises, as long as proper ventilation is provided.

The principal is the primary contact for parents who want to know what the renovations will entail. He or she should let parents know well in advance what will be done and when so they can prepare their children for what to expect, both from a safety standpoint and an emotional one. If you have not been kept up-to-date by the administration, you have every right to request complete access to all plans.

Families should emphasize the need to keep a positive attitude about the many inconveniences involved in renovating a school, just as they would if their home was undergoing remodeling or renovation. On the other hand, it is also important for the safety-minded parent to watch the proceedings personally. The principal should have a "phasing plan" that has been agreed on and accepted by the contractors and the school, specifying which rooms will be worked on and when. This plan should be available for any parent to view at any time.

By law, there must be two exits from any floor of the school at all times, especially during renovations. This is usually no problem on the main floor, but is something to be aware of on the second floor and up. To maintain the two exits on floors above ground level, workers shouldn't erect impassable barriers. Therefore, they will most likely use yellow tape or wooden barriers that are easy to remove in an emergency. However, these are the kinds of "flimsy" barriers that attract children's curiosity, so children must be cautioned to respect them.

It's nice if the school can use the renovations as a learning experience, because this is the best way to insure safety. When workers visit classrooms and show children the tools being used and explain what the yellow tape is for, children are more likely to obey the safety rules, in addition to learning about and enjoying the process of renovation.

▼ ▼

FOUR RENOVATION RULES FOR CHILDREN

What safety instructions should you give your children regarding renovations at school? Here are four suggestions from Doris Cole, president of Cole & Goyette Architecture and Planners Inc., whose firm renovates many schools in the Boston area:[13]

1. Obey the safety instructions your principal and teachers give you. If you don't understand what to do, ask your teacher.

2. Respect the barriers workers use to keep people away from certain areas. These might be large wooden barriers or pieces of tape stretched across a hallway. They are meant to keep you from getting hurt. Never climb or jump over a barrier or tear it down.

3. Never enter a work area that has been closed off. If a sign says "Keep Out," don't go in!

4. Do not touch any materials or tools being used by workers.

▼ ▼

Architecture: Getting Involved from the Ground Up

Parents can and should get involved in the process if a new school is being planned in their community or an older one is being renovated. So should teachers. "It remains a radical idea to most architects in public projects to talk to the people who will use what they build, instead of just to those agencies who will hire them," says Troy West, an architect.[14] This trend is well enough recognized to be called "participatory design" or "advocacy planning."

If you have the happy opportunity to collaborate on a new school in your community, you may want to look into the following safety-related architectural issues.[15] Be aware that very often, safety and aesthetic concerns do not coincide. Safety should always take precedence.

▶ *Building codes.* Schools are affected by three building codes: basic, state, and regional. They are also affected by Americans with Disabilities Act (ADA) codes, health codes, and fire codes. While you probably can't know all the details of every code, you certainly can ask a lot of questions.

▶ *Restrooms.* The size and location of student restrooms affect students' safety. For bathrooms to be well-supervised, they should be close enough to classrooms for teachers to check on them easily. Even better is a restroom in each classroom. Bathrooms should be large enough to accommodate the student population, and girls' bathrooms should be larger than boys'.

▶ *Hallways.* These should be wide enough to prevent crowding, which leads to discipline problems (bumping encourages antisocial behavior). Enough space should be allocated for lockers so halls will still be wide enough. There should be no alcoves where students can congregate and hide.

▶ *Cafeterias.* Should be large enough to accommodate the entire school population.

▶ *Stairways.* Should accommodate large numbers of students going up and down. Railings should not allow students to throw things. Railings should be the correct height for the ages of the students.

▶ *"Parents' room."* One room should officially be designated a "parents' room."

▶ *Outside access.* Rooms that will be used by the public either during or after school hours, like auditoriums, gyms, and libraries, should be designed with outside access so that other parts of the building do not need to be entered.

▶ *Air conditioning:* The new/renovated school should definitely have air conditioning. See pages 143–144.

▶ *Windows.* There should be swing-away window guards over windows so glass doesn't get broken and students can't fall out. Windows should be able to be opened for ventilation. Smaller window panes are easier than large ones to replace if broken.

▸ *Preschool programs.* If a preschool program is also located in the school, their area should be separate and on the ground level.

▸ *Lighting.* Attention should be paid to getting natural light in as many rooms as possible.

▸ *Physically challenged students.* Requirements for the Americans with Disabilities Act (ADA) to accommodate physically challenged students make schools safer for all students.

▸ *Shop and art supply areas.* Enough space must be allocated to these so they are not crowded and dangerous materials can be stored safely.

▸ *Labs.* All labs should meet Occupational Safety and Health Administration (OSHA) requirements.

▸ *Wiring.* Extra wiring should be planned for to accommodate future electrical needs.

▸ *Parking.* Enough parking should be planned, including for times when the community uses the school on weekends, etc.

▸ *Drop-off and pick-up.* A clear and safe drop-off and pick-up traffic lane should be planned. The lane should be long enough for all buses to line up. A separate lane should be made for cars.

▸ *Fire safety.* Aspects of fire safety include compartmentalization (fire safety doors) to prevent fire from spreading, a sprinkler system, early warning systems, and adequate exits.

▸ *Security.* The school should be designed to be secure from outsiders. Staff in the front office should be able to see the entrance. Play areas should be enclosed.

7

Physical and Mental Health

▼ ▼

Six-year-old Ellen is on medication, and she needs to take a pill every three hours. How can her parents make sure that she'll take her medicine on time? Nine-year-old Robert seems depressed lately. Is there anyone at school who can help? Marie hates her junior-high history class. The boy who sits behind her has been calling her names and touching her when the teacher isn't looking. Marie's parents are concerned that their daughter is being sexually harassed.

These are just a few of the countless questions parents may have regarding their children's physical and mental health while at school. When your kids are at home, you can make sure that their health needs are attended to. While you can't ask teachers to wipe your children's noses or give them the same constant attention you would, there are many things that you as a parent can request and do to make school safer and healthier for your children.

The School Nurse

The school nurse is on the front lines of school safety. He or she sees all the injuries, physical and emotional, that students present. If the nurse is on staff full-time, he or she has a wonderful opportunity to get to know the children and to observe and diagnose any problems.

State guidelines vary on school nurse duties. In general, besides treating minor cuts and bruises, the school nurse is involved with immunization, child abuse, sexual abuse, AIDS, neglect, special needs, student mental health, Lyme disease, lice, eating disorders, tuberculosis, substance abuse, family life education, teen pregnancy, and identifying and assessing all of these and more.

Asthma and diabetes are two conditions that often need the aid of the school nurse. According to the U.S. Department of Health and Human Services, effective asthma management at school can help to:[1]

▶ promote a supportive learning environment for students with asthma

▶ reduce absences

▶ reduce disruption in the classroom

▶ provide necessary support in the event of an emergency.

In addition, it can help children with asthma achieve full participation in physical activities so they don't feel "left out" and self-conscious about their asthma. One of the most important roles of the school nurse is to explain to a child's class about major problems a child has—say, seizures or injuries that need dressing changes—so classmates understand the student's needs and don't ostracize him or her.

The policy statement of the National Association of School Nurses (NASN) states that nurses provide health assessments, develop and implement health plans, maintain data, assist in the control of communicable diseases, provide health education, and act as liaisons between the school and community.[2] The school nurse can also be the eyes and ears of the parent, so if you are worried about sending your child to school when she may not be feeling well but not sick enough to stay home, ask the nurse to check up on her.

▼ ▼

FIVE WAYS YOU CAN HELP YOUR SCHOOL NURSE

1. Make sure that your child's immunizations are complete and up-to-date. You will need to have your pediatrician fill out a school health form on a regular basis listing your child's immunizations and dates.

2. If your child has allergies or other health problems, tell the nurse about them. Discuss any special needs such as no furry pets in the classroom, physical education limitations, etc.

3. Inform the nurse about what to do if your child is injured at school and you can't be reached. Fill out the spaces on your school health form naming people to contact and giving their daytime telephone numbers.

4. When the nurse sends home information about health issues, read it carefully. If you have questions, ask. Request additional information about health issues that concern you.

5. Encourage the nurse or another health professional to train students and staff in basic emergency lifesaving techniques. For example, older students can be taught CPR.

▼ ▼

Schools without Nurses

The role of the school nurse is vital to children's safety, but it is not one that is deemed necessary in many schools. Although some schools do have full-time school nurses, and others have full-scale on-site health clinics, thousands of schools have no nurse on staff at all.

According to Elaine Taboskey, president of the National Association of School Nurses (NASN), there are only 26,000 school nurses in the United States.[3] Yet there are over 83,000 schools.[4] That leaves over half of our schools without on-campus medical assistance. Compounding the problem is a shortage of school nurses in some areas of the country due to the low pay and low status associated with the job.

The absence of professional health care in schools causes many problems, both minor and serious. For example, an elementary school in Nevada that employs only a part-time school nurse gave the job of administering student medication to an aide on the nurse's day off. The aide called two boys into the office from their classes, and with both children in front of her, she administered medicine to one of them. When she checked the bottle for the next child, however, she realized her mistake. She had given the first boy cerebral palsy medication instead of asthma medication! Frantic, she called 911, and the boy was rushed to the hospital to have his stomach pumped. He's doing fine, physically, but the emotional scars remaining on the boy and the aide will last a long time.[5]

Annie Barclay, president of the Educational Support Employees Association, is angry about the health care situation in our schools. "Parents should recognize that there are hundreds of employees other than teachers," she emphasizes, "and should demand that these employees have the training and resources they need."[6] Parents should be deeply concerned if their children need to take medication in school but there is no one qualified to give it. Schools need full-time health practitioners, yet they are increasingly eliminating this position from the staff when budgets are cut. Aides are fearful of doing jobs like administering medication for which they are not qualified, and nurses are concerned that children are not getting the care they need.

If there is no nurse at your children's school, work with your parent group to remedy this situation. Start by calling your state Department of Education to find out the law regarding school nurses in your state. Some states require nurses, but most don't. Elaine Taboskey of the NASN suggests that you join forces with parents of children with special needs, as these parents often have considerable experience advocating for their children's health.[7] In some states, certain nursing procedures can be funded by Medicaid. Don't be surprised if you hear administrators say, "We don't need a school nurse; we only have well children here." Be prepared to combat this misconception with anecdotal or factual information about the health needs of the students in your school that are not being met. For advice, support, and additional information, call your local Department of Health.

▼ ▼

IF YOUR CHILD MUST TAKE MEDICATION AT SCHOOL...

1. Provide the school with written orders from a physician. These written orders should include the name of the medication, the dosage, and the time intervals at which your child should take it.

2. Request in writing that the school comply with the doctor's orders.

3. Bring medication to school in the original container. Check to make sure it is properly labeled.

4. Give the initial dose at home. That way you can notice any side effects. The initial dose should be given at school only under life-threatening conditions.

5. Ask the school to record in a log each dose given.

6. Ask the school nurse to inform other appropriate staff members about the benefits and side effects of your child's medication. This includes your child's teacher(s).

7. Confirm that the medication will be stored in a locked cabinet at all times.

Understand that school personnel have the right to refuse to administer medication if they feel unqualified to do so—for example, if there is no school nurse. You can ask a teacher or aide to do it, but staff are entitled to decline. Parents can come to school and give the medication themselves if necessary.

▼ ▼

The School Counselor

Some schools have school psychologists and/or counselors on staff, whether full-time or part-time. Students go to them for help with personal problems, often because they can't or won't talk to their parents. The right school counselor can do a lot to help students feel safe at school.

There used to be a larger distinction between guidance counselors and counselors that helped students with personal problems. In many schools, that distinction remains, but in others, guidance counselors—originally hired to guide students with course, college, and career choices—find themselves doing less of that and more emotional and social intervention.

School counselors can help children with school- and career-related decisions, as well as help them deal with personal problems like their parents' divorce, abuse, drug and alcohol abuse, suicide prevention, attendance, nutrition, and much more.

If your child is having school-related problems or family problems affecting his or her school work, make an appointment to talk to the school counselor. It's free! Be sure to make allowances for the counselor's busy schedule, especially if he or she is only part-time at your school. Also, keep in mind that the school counselor cannot be your personal family therapist. He or she may have hundreds of students or several schools to serve. If the counselor feels that you need more help than can be provided in a meeting or two, he or she may refer you to a professional in private practice for further counseling.

If your child has learning needs that you feel are not being properly addressed, talk to the counselor. He or she can arrange for testing to help determine whether your child is gifted, learning disabled (or "learning different"), or qualified to receive special help in other areas.

For a catalog of counseling publications, write or call:

- American School Counselor Association
  c/o American Counseling Association
  5999 Stevenson Avenue
  Alexandria, VA 22304-3300
  Toll-free telephone: 1-800-347-6647

▼ ▼

SUICIDE AWARENESS AND PREVENTION

Suicide among young people is on the rise, and school counselors can play an important role in keeping children from killing themselves. A counselor who is truly "in touch" with students can be a confidant for kids who have no one else to talk to. The counselor can also help to educate students about the warning signs of suicide and what to do if they recognize these signs in their friends—or in themselves.

Find out what your school is doing about suicide awareness and prevention. Is this topic addressed anywhere in the curriculum? How is it addressed? Ask what plans are in place in the event that a student commits suicide. For example, is the school prepared to provide grief counseling? Have teachers and other staff members been sensitized to the needs of suicide survivors—the friends who are left behind, and who may be feeling responsible for the suicide? ("If only I had done something....If only I had paid attention....If only I hadn't said what I did....")

For more information about suicide, suicide awareness, and suicide prevention, write or call:

- The American Association of Suicidology
  2459 South Ash
  Denver, CO 80222
  Telephone: (303) 692-0985

Students can be active suicide preventers. *The Power to Prevent Suicide: A Guide for Teens Helping Teens* by Dr. Richard A. Nelson and Judith C. Galas (Free Spirit Publishing, 1994) tells teens how to recognize the warning signs and get help for suicidal friends. For more information, call Free Spirit Publishing toll-free at 1-800-735-7323.

When a Friend Dies: A Book for Teens about Grieving & Healing by Marilyn Gootman, Ed.D. (Free Spirit Publishing, 1994) can help students cope with the sadness and trauma of a peer suicide. Contact Free Spirit at the number above.

▼ ▼

AIDS Awareness and Prevention

Schools across the United States are currently deciding what to do about AIDS awareness and prevention. Some will ultimately determine that they don't want to be involved with it at all, leaving the responsibility to parents, medical professionals, and other health officials. Others will choose to offer AIDS awareness and prevention education in varying degrees.

The National Education Association recommends that all schools establish an AIDS awareness and prevention curriculum. This would typically include information on how HIV (the AIDS virus) is transmitted, what behaviors are known to put individuals at risk for contracting HIV, and how to avoid putting oneself at risk.

If your children's school decides to teach AIDS awareness and prevention, this should be handled as a health issue, not a moral issue. AIDS educators should receive special training, and parents should be informed and consulted about the program. Contact your local American Red Cross chapter or your state or local health department for information and advice on AIDS curricula.

Whether your children's school teaches about AIDS or not, you should make sure that your children know the facts about AIDS. Newspapers and magazines often print articles about AIDS; these are a good source of up-to-date information. Ask your pediatrician to give you brochures or other printed materials about AIDS. Visit your library and check out these books to share with your child:

▸ *What's a Virus, Anyway? The Kids' Book about AIDS* by David Fassler, M.D., and Kelly McQueen (Burlington, VT: Waterfront Books, 1990). A brief, clear explanation of a frightening subject, suitable for elementary school age children.

▸ *Risky Times: How To Be AIDS Smart and Stay Healthy* by Jeanne Blake (New York: Workman Publishing, 1990). Appropriate for middle school, this book features famous and ordinary people talking about AIDS, with no explicit photographs or drawings.

▸ *AIDS: Trading Fears for Facts: A Guide for Young People*, updated edition by Karen Hein, M.D. (Yonkers, NY: Consumer Reports Books, 1991). This is the nitty-gritty, with explicit drawings and tell-all text. For high school.

▼ ▼

FIND OUT MORE ABOUT AIDS

▸ Call one or both of the toll-free National AIDS Hotlines operated by the Public Health Service. Call 1-800-342-AIDS (1-800-342-2437) to speak to a hotline staff person. Free written materials are available on request.

▸ Order free materials about AIDS from the Centers for Disease Control (CDC). Call toll-free: 1-800-458-5231.

▸ Request the free booklet, "AIDS and the Education of Our Children." Write to:

   ◦ Consumer Information Center
    Department ED
    Pueblo, CO 81009

▸ Through its AIDS Public Education Program, the American Red Cross distributes educational materials to local Red Cross chapters throughout the United States. Contact your local chapter.

▼ ▼

Children with AIDS

Is it safe for your children to attend school with an HIV-positive child? Yes, because the risk of transmitting the virus is almost nonexistent.[8] Since in most cases children with HIV are allowed by law to attend school, it's important to reassure your children that there is no danger involved.

The U.S. Department of Education notes that:[9]

▸ "Children with AIDS are handicapped persons.... Section 504 [of the Education of the Handicapped Act] prohibits discrimination against persons with handicaps in federally assisted programs such as elementary and secondary schools."

▸ "Most children with AIDS can attend school in the regular classroom without restrictions."

▸ "A child with AIDS has a right to confidentiality."

However, the Department recommends that children with full-blown AIDS who lack control over their bodily functions, have open cuts or wounds, or display behaviors such as biting receive instruction *outside* the classroom.[10] Information on who has AIDS is generally confidential and may not be released, but the specific laws on this vary from state to state and from case to case. You will want to be sure to monitor developments in your state.

State and local school districts need to form their own policies on students and staff with HIV. Parents can and should be involved in this process. There is a very helpful book available that your parent group may want to purchase. Titled *Someone at School Has AIDS*, this guide to developing policies for students and staff members who are infected with HIV is available for $10.50 (the cost at the time of this writing) from:

> National Association of State Boards of Education
> 1012 Cameron Street
> Alexandria, VA 22314
> Telephone: (703) 684-4000

In this book, you will find guidelines like the following:[11]

▸ "Barring special circumstances, students who are infected with HIV shall attend the school and classroom to which they would be assigned if they were not affected. They are entitled to all rights, privileges, and services accorded to other students."

▸ "Since HIV is not transmitted through behaviors that are permitted at school, the identity of a student or staff member who is infected with HIV need not be shared with many people.... The family may wish to notify a principal, teacher, or other staff member...but no one needs to know."

Children with AIDS have a weakened immune system and will react more seriously to common childhood illnesses, so it's best all around if they are constantly reassessed as to whether they should remain in school. Any child with AIDS should be under a doctor's supervision.

Common Sense and Universal Precautions

It's common sense to warn our children not to touch another person's blood, urine, or other body fluids with their bare hands. Since cuts, scrapes, nosebleeds, and vomiting are everyday occurrences in schools, this advice is critical—and not only because of AIDS. Other diseases, including hepatitis, can be transmitted via body fluids.

"One of the most important issues parents should look into is whether nurses, custodians, physical education teachers, and coaches are trained in and are using Universal Precautions when body fluids are spilled," says Elaine Taboskey of the National Association of School Nurses.[12] "Universal Precautions" means that *everyone* must follow precautions as if *everyone* involved has an infectious disease like AIDS or hepatitis. If an injury happens during a football game, for example, the game must be stopped until the blood is cleaned up by the custodian and disposed of properly.

Find out if your school follows Universal Precautions. Are the necessary supplies available, including latex gloves? Do school staff members have access to the supplies, and have they been trained to use them? How are medical wastes handled and disposed of?

A videotape on Universal Precautions titled "It's Up to You" is available for $8.00 (the cost at the time of this writing) from:

- AIDS Education Project
  American Federation of Teachers
  555 NJ Avenue, N.W.
  Washington, DC 20001
  Toll-free telephone: 1-800-238-1133

Although this video is from the teacher's point of view, it describes many excellent procedures. If parents can get these procedures adopted in their schools, staff *and* students will be protected.

For more information on Universal Precautions, contact your local Occupational Safety and Health Administration (OSHA) office or your local health department.

Sex Education

Most people agree that schools should teach sex education, but they disagree over when to introduce it and what it should involve. Regarding timing, many experts say that sex education should be presented by or before middle school; high school is too late.[13] Regarding content, society is currently debating whether sex education classes should stress abstinence vs. contraception, whether condoms should be distributed in schools, and whether and to what extent AIDS awareness and prevention should be part of the curriculum.

But while adults are debating these issues, young people are getting pregnant and contracting HIV. Each year, more than one million teenagers—one in nine girls ages 15 to 19—become pregnant.[14] And there were 800 new AIDS cases among children 13 years of age and younger in 1992, up from 400 in 1987.[15]

To find out how your school is dealing with these complex and controversial issues, start by asking for a copy of your school's sex education curriculum. Read it carefully. Find out if the teacher has had special training in sex education, and talk to him or her about any concerns you have. Most importantly, discuss sex frankly with your children, provide them with books on sex and human sexuality, and communicate your personal and family values to them on a regular basis.

Here are some excellent sex education books you may want to share with your children:

▸ *Your Body, Yourself* by Alison Bell and Lisa Rooney, M.D. (Los Angeles: Lowell House Juvenile Books, 1993). Good information for children in upper elementary and middle school.

▸ *The What's Happening to My Body? Book for Boys*, New Edition, by Lynda Madaras with Dane Saavedra and *The What's Happening to My Body? Book for Girls*, New Edition, by Lynda Madaras with Area Madaras (both New York: Newmarket Press, 1988). Straight talk for high school students.

Condoms in Schools

Opponents of condom distribution in schools say that it will give students permission to be sexually active. They fear that it may imply that condoms are a foolproof defense against AIDS and pregnancy, which they are not.

Supporters of condom distribution say that teenage pregnancy and AIDS are public health crises that must be brought under control by whatever means possible. They believe that condom distribution should be part of a comprehensive sex education program that includes discussion of abstinence.

Whatever you feel personally about these issues, make sure that your children know the facts about AIDS and pregnancy. See page 120 and above for descriptions of age-appropriate books. Above all, be willing to talk to your kids about these vital issues. Listen to their concerns, try to answer their questions, and get help when you don't have answers. Be glad if your children are coming to you for information and advice.

Sexual Abuse

Sexual abuse is widespread in our society, and children at school are not immune. Students are being sexually abused by other students and even by teachers and other staff members. Experts in child abuse say that pedophiles (deviant adults who seek out sex with children) are naturally attracted to schools.

Often, sexual abuse is discovered long after it occurs. There may be many reasons why children don't report it. Some fear that no one would believe them if they told. Some feel that they have no one they can tell about this terrible thing that is happening to them. Some believe that they are responsible for the abuse—that it is somehow their fault. Some are too confused and ashamed to tell. Some are afraid for their lives or the lives of their loved ones because the abuser has threatened retaliation if they tell.

Sexual abuse happens everywhere—in public schools and private schools, "good" schools and "bad" schools, even in churches. The best way to protect your children from abuse is with a combination of awareness, education, and vigilant attention. Here's what you can do:

▶ Teach your children that they do not have to absolutely obey adults, school personnel, older students, or other authority figures just because they're in charge. Explain that they need to obey school rules, but they also have the right to ask questions and to say no to things they sense or know to be wrong.

▶ Tell them to trust their instincts. If someone makes them "feel funny," or if someone tries to touch them in ways that feel strange, wrong, or scary, they should get away as fast as they can and tell another adult.

▶ Take note of anyone at school (or anywhere else) who seems to be too interested in your children for any reason.

▶ Examine your school's policy on hiring volunteers. Often, volunteers are not screened as thoroughly as paid employees. While you're at it, examine the policies of after-school groups including day care programs and scouting. Between 1971 and 1991, some 1,800 scoutmasters suspected of molesting boys were removed by the Boy Scouts of America. Organization files show that some simply went elsewhere.[16]

▸ Listen closely if your children say that someone at school frightens them or they "don't like" a certain school staff member. Even if they can't articulate what's wrong, you should follow through and find out more.

If a child tells you about an abuse incident, try to find out as much as you can. Listen supportively, but don't put words into the child's mouth. Let the child tell the story in his or her own words, and believe the child.[17]

After hearing of your child's traumatic experience, there are several people you should contact—in this order:

▸ Your pediatrician or family doctor.

▸ The school principal, who is one of a number of "mandated reporters" who are required to contact the police. (Teachers are "mandated reporters," too.)

▸ The police. Although the principal is required by law to contact the police, you should also do this yourself. The police will then decide who will investigate and how the investigation will be done.

▸ A child therapist. State and county divisions of youth and family services can be helpful as well.

You might also want to contact the following organization:

⬤ National Committee for the Prevention of Child Abuse
200 State Road
South Deerfield, MA 01373-0200
Toll-free telephone: 1-800-835-2671

Almost every state requires teachers to report "evidence of serious physical or mental injury."[18] This means that teachers must report all suspected abuse of a child by anyone. Most states provide criminal penalties to school personnel for failure to report abuse. All states provide immunity from any liability for reporting such actions, unless the reports were intentionally false.

Sexual Harassment

Sexual harassment in schools became the focus of national attention in 1989, when Minnesota passed a groundbreaking law requiring school boards in the state to have written policies on sexual harassment. This law came about partly as a result of a legal action by a student named Katy Lyle. Katy was a 15-

year-old high school student when vulgar and degrading graffiti about her began appearing in one of the boys' bathrooms. She complained to the school, but nothing was done. She sued and eventually settled for $15,000.

In 1993, a study commissioned by the American Association of University Women (AAUW) Educational Foundation reported that breast-grabbing, sexual jokes, and sexual teasing are common and considered "normal" teenage behaviors.[19] The study, titled *Hostile Hallways*, concluded that sexual harassment is an enormous problem in our schools, and that "parents, teachers, and administrators must acknowledge that sexual harassment in school is creating a hostile environment that compromises the education of America's children.... Although girls are experiencing more harassment, in the end sexual harassment is everyone's problem. For when children's self-esteem and development are hampered, the repercussions echo throughout our society."

Other key findings from the AAUW report include:

▸ Sexual harassment is widespread: 81% of girls and boys have experienced it.

▸ Sexual comments, jokes, looks, and gestures— as well as touching, grabbing, and/or pinching in a sexual way—are commonplace in schools: 66% of the students surveyed had been targets of these.

▸ The third most common form of sexual harassment in schools (after sexual comments and touching) involves intentionally brushing up against someone in a sexual way—something girls experience far more often than boys.

▸ Notably higher numbers of girls than boys say they have suffered as a result of sexual harassment in school; African-American girls have suffered the most.

▸ Boys routinely experience harassment, too; among African-American boys, the incidence of harassment involving direct physical contact is alarming.

The most frequent forms of sexual harassment in schools are student-to-student and teacher-to-student, although it is also possible for students to harass teachers by making sexual advances. Sexual harassment may be male-to-female, female-to-female, female-to-male, and male-to-male.

What Is Sexual Harassment?

Sexual harassment can be verbal, nonverbal, and/or physical. The AAUW report names several behaviors that are considered to be sexually harassing. All have two things in common: they are sexually related, and they are unwanted by the person being harassed. These behaviors include:[20]

▶   staring up and down

▶   spreading sexual gossip

▶   blocking or cornering in a sexual way

▶   spying while changing at gym

▶   sexual gestures

▶   sexual jokes

▶   sexual written letters

▶   pulling at clothes (skirts up, pants down, bra pulling, others)

▶   pulling off clothes

▶   comments about genitals or sex

▶   sexual rumors

▶   sexual graffiti

▶   "flashing" or "mooning"

▶   asking questions about one's sexual experience

▶   a reward of good grades from a teacher in return for sexual favors

▶   pinup posters hung up anywhere in school

▶   showing, giving, or leaving around sexual pictures, photographs, illustrations, messages, or notes

▶   sexual touching, grabbing, or pinching

▶   grabbing or fondling genitals

▶   forced kissing

▶   rape and other sexual assaults.

Confusion exists about the difference between flirting and sexual harassment. When Dr. Nan Stein, director of the Sexual Harassment in Schools Project at Wellesley College, spoke with high school girls about this issue, the girls told her that comments like "Hi, honey, what's up?" and "Nice skirt" were flirtatious. But remarks like "Big butt, can I grab it?" and "Your breasts are a 10" were considered sexually harassing.[21]

Except for blatantly obvious behaviors, sexual harassment often is in the eye (or ear) of the beholder—the person being harassed. What matters is how that person *feels*. Students surveyed over a period of years reported the following differences between flirting and sexual harassment:[22]

▶ Flirting makes the receiver feel good, happy, flattered, attractive, and in control. Sexual harassment makes the receiver feel bad, angry, sad, demeaned, ugly, and powerless.

▶ Flirting boosts the receiver's self-esteem. Sexual harassment damages the receiver's self-esteem.

▶ Flirting is wanted and equality-motivated. Sexual harassment is unwanted and power-motivated.

▼ ▼

SEXUAL HARASSMENT AND THE LAW

There is another important difference between flirting and sexual harassment: Flirting is *legal*, but sexual harassment is *illegal*. Specifically:

▶ Sexual harassment in schools is illegal according to Civil Rights Act Title IX of the Federal Education Amendments, which prohibits sexual harassment in education.

▶ In 1992, the United States Supreme Court unanimously ruled that students who suffer sexual harassment and other forms of sex discrimination can seek monetary damages from their schools and school officials for violating their civil rights.

▶ Sexual harassment may also be a criminal offense under child abuse laws.

▼ ▼

What You Can Do about Sexual Harassment

Too often, educators, parents, and students trivialize sexual harassment. They ignore it, say that the harasser "didn't mean it," claim that the victim "misinterpreted it," dismiss it as "typical teenage behavior" or, if boys are doing the harassing, excuse it as just another way in which "boys will be boys." But sexual harassment is a serious problem in our schools, with harmful effects on everyone, and we need to take it seriously. Here's what you can do:

1. *Talk to your children about sexual harassment.* Make sure they understand that certain behaviors are unacceptable—at school or anywhere else. Discuss with them the behaviors listed on page 128. Ask if they can give other examples of behaviors that might be considered sexual harassment.

2. *Help your children understand the difference between right and wrong things to say and do.* Teach them to ask themselves these simple questions:[23]

▸   Is this something I would want my family and friends to know I had said or done?

▸   Is this something I would say or do around my parents? Around my girlfriend/boyfriend?

▸   Is this something I would want someone else to say or do to my mother/father, sister/brother, girlfriend/boyfriend?

▸   Is this something I would say or do if the other person's parents or boyfriend/girlfriend were present?

3. *Help your children understand how to tell if they are being sexually harassed.* You might offer this explanation: "If someone says something to you or touches you in a way that makes you feel bad, embarrassed, scared, or uncomfortable, that person could be sexually harassing you." Encourage your children to tell you about any incidents that feel "wrong" to them. Listen to your children. Write down what they say, complete with names, times, dates, and circumstances.

4. *If your school has a procedure in place for reporting sexual harassment, use it.* If your school doesn't have a procedure in place, work with other parents and school staff to establish one. Meanwhile, report any and all incidents to the teacher, guidance counselor, or principal.

5. *If you believe that your child has been harassed, and if telling the school doesn't get results, contact your state department of education to file a formal complaint.*

6. *Ask your school to offer workshops and training sessions for students and staff on sexual harassment awareness, prevention, and reporting.* Contact your state department of education to request workshop and training materials.

Sexual Harassment and Teens: A Program for Positive Change by Susan Strauss (Free Spirit Publishing, 1992) is a course in sexual harassment designed for grades 7 through 12. It brings people together to explore and understand the causes and consequences of sexual harassment, helps participants to identify sexual harassment problems that may exist in their school, and explains how to design a sexual harassment policy, develop formal and informal grievance procedures, and create a healthy, respectful learning and working environment for students and staff. The curriculum has three units that may be presented in three class periods of about 45 to 60 minutes. For more information, call Free Spirit Publishing toll-free: 1-800-735-7323.

Alcohol and Other Drugs

In the schoolyard, the restroom, the cafeteria, and even in the classroom, your child *will* be approached and invited to try alcohol and other drugs. Will they resist, or will they join in? Consider that by the eighth grade:[24]

▸ 70% of children have tried alcohol

▸ 10% have tried marijuana

▸ 2% have used cocaine.

In addition, children are even inhaling common household chemicals like butane, glue, solvents, and correction fluid.[25] Clearly, *all* parents must be on the alert to the possibility that their children are using alcohol and illegal drugs.

▼ ▼

FIVE SIGNS THAT A STUDENT MAY BE ABUSING ALCOHOL AND/OR OTHER DRUGS

A student who is abusing alcohol and/or other drugs may:

1. display changes in mood and/or attitude that negatively affect family and friend relationships. Arguments and secrecy become common.

2. neglect school work and begin to skip classes or days of school.

3. resist discipline at home and school.

4. borrow and/or steal money from family, friends, and school.

5. drop old friends and develop a new group of friends—other students who abuse alcohol and/or other drugs.

▼ ▼

How to Help Your Children Say No to Alcohol and Other Drugs

1. *Talk with your children about peer pressure and how to resist it.* Look for books on resisting peer pressure at your bookstore and library and role-play the scenarios they suggest. A recommendation:

▶ *Peer Pressure Reversal: An Adult Guide to Developing a Responsible Child* by Sharon Scott (Amherst, MA: Human Resource Development Press, 1987). Great role-playing ideas to teach children how to act and what to say when caught in a "peer-engineered trap."

2. *Talk with your children about alcohol and other drugs.* Start by educating yourself. Contact any or all of the following to request information:

▶ National Institute on Drug Abuse; toll-free telephone: 1-800-662-HELP (1-800-662-4357)

▶ National Clearinghouse for Alcohol and Drug Information; toll-free telephone: 1-800-729-6686

▸ U.S. Department of Education; toll-free telephone: 1-800-624-0100 (Request copies of the free booklets, "Schools without Drugs," "Growing Up Drug-Free," and "Prevention Plus II")

▸ Al-Anon; toll-free telephone: 1-800-344-2666

▸ Alcoholics Anonymous; check your Yellow Pages under "Alcoholics" for a chapter near you

▸ Cocaine Helpline; toll-free telephone: 1-800-COCAINE (1-800-262-2463).

3. *Help your children to develop positive self-esteem.* Strengthen their self-esteem at home by treating them with respect and showing them every day that you love them and value them. Look for books on self-esteem at your bookstore and library. Recommendations:

▸ *How to Give Your Child a Great Self-Image: Proven Techniques to Build Confidence from Infancy to Adolescence* by Dr. Debra Phillips with Fred Bernstein (New York: Penguin, 1991). A behavioral therapist offers role-playing ideas to parents on how to avoid destructive language and use positive reinforcement instead.

▸ *Stick Up For Yourself! Every Kid's Guide to Personal Power and Positive Self-Esteem* by Gershen Kaufman, Ph.D., and Lev Raphael, Ph.D. (Free Spirit Publishing, 1990). Realistic, encouraging how-to advice on being assertive, building relationships, and becoming responsible. For ages 8–12, but much good advice for all ages (including adults). Also available: *A Teacher's Guide to Stick Up For Yourself: A 10-Part Course in Self-Esteem and Assertiveness for Kids* by Gerri Johnson, Gershen Kaufman, and Lev Raphael. You may want to suggest that your school offer a "Stick Up For Yourself!" course for kids using these books. For more information, call Free Spirit Publishing toll-free: 1-800-735-7323.

4. *Be a good role model.* Many adults use alcohol responsibly and in moderation. Those who abuse alcohol or other drugs are setting a poor example for their children.

5. *Keep your children so busy with life that they don't have time for alcohol or other drugs.* Involve them in a variety of activities—lessons, clubs, sports, community service.

6. *Know where they are and who they are with.* Have you met your children's friends? Are they welcome at your house? When you let your children visit their

friends or go to parties, do you make sure in advance that there will be adult supervision? Have you met the parents of your children's friends? The more you know about your children's social life, the better. And if their friends are welcome at your house, then *you* can provide the supervision.

7.   *Form a parent network.* Members agree to chaperone their children's parties, make sure that any student gatherings at their homes are alcohol- and drug-free, and communicate with one another about their children's activities. You might formalize this network by printing a brochure explaining its purpose, outlining the members' responsibilities, and listing their names and telephone numbers. Forming a parent network is an excellent project for your parent group.

How You Can Influence School Curricula and Policies Regarding Alcohol and Other Drugs

Most of the information your children receive about alcohol and other drugs will come from school curricula, provided their schools offer such curricula. As of 1987, the most recent figures available, only 39 states require substance abuse education, only 32 provide minimum standards, only 11 require certification in substance abuse education for all teachers, and only 17 have adopted or designed prevention curricula.[26]

If your school offers substance abuse education, ask to see a copy of the curriculum. Read it carefully to make sure it's up-to-date. Older programs focus on feelings, self-esteem, and personal experiences. These are not prevention programs, they are social skills programs. Other programs put teachers in counseling roles for which they are not prepared. Newer, more effective programs use role-playing to give students concrete practice in resisting peer pressure.

The Alcohol, Drug Abuse, and Mental Health Administration gives the following guidelines for substance abuse curricula in its publication, "Prevention Plus II":[27]

1.   *The material should give a clear no-use message.* Even small amounts of alcohol and/or other drugs increase injury and health risks. (In other words, "just a sip" is not okay for minors.)

2. *The material should make it clear that illegal drug use is unhealthy and harmful for all persons.* This includes the use of any legally prohibited drug; use of a legal drug for other than its intended use; use of a product that can produce a drug-like effect (glue, aerosols); and use of a legal drug (including alcohol or tobacco) by individuals legally underage.

There are two red-flag phrases to look for in unacceptable material:

▶   "mood-altering" as a euphemism for mind-altering

▶   any implication that there are no "good" or "bad" drugs, just improper use, misuse, or abuse.

3. *The material should make it clear that young people are responsible for their own decisions.* It should not provide opportunities for them to make excuses for their behavior.

4. *The material should not use illustrations or dramatizations that could teach people how to obtain, prepare, or ingest illegal drugs.*

5. *The information contained in the material should be scientifically accurate and up-to-date.*

6. *The material should be appropriate for the developmental age, interests, and needs of the students.*

7. *The material should not contain racist or sexist biases, either blatant or subtle.*

8. *The material should not use recovering addicts or alcoholics as role models.* "Prevention education materials that use recovering addicts or alcoholics as role models do not conform to Office for Substance Abuse Prevention and Department of Education policy. Focus group testing has shown that children enrolled in prevention education programs may get a different message from what is intended from the testimony of recovering addicts. Rather than the intended 'don't do as I did' message, children may hear the message that the speaker used drugs and survived very well or even became wealthy and famous. An exception may be for role models who clearly show that they have been negatively affected by the use of alcohol another drugs, such as someone now *visibly* handicapped or injured."[28]

Use these guidelines to evaluate your school's current policy on alcohol/drug awareness and prevention, or to approach administrators about initiating a policy if one does not already exist. "Prevention Plus II" recommends the following procedure:[29]

1. *Schools should have a means of determining the extent of alcohol and other drug use on school premises.* One way to do this is by:

▶   surveying students, parents, and administrators about alcohol and other drug use, and

▶   maintaining records of abuses, parent meetings, and consultations with school personnel to determine areas where alcohol and other drugs are being used and sold on school premises.

2. *Schools should establish clear and specific rules regarding the use of alcohol and other drugs on school grounds or at school functions.* The rules should state that the use of alcohol and other drugs by students and staff will not be tolerated. They should cover prevention, intervention, treatment, and disciplinary measures, and they should specify what constitutes an offense by defining:

▶   items that should not be brought to school (alcohol, illegal drugs, and paraphernalia)

▶   the areas of the school's jurisdiction (school property, its surroundings, and all school-related events)

▶   the types of violations (possession, use, sale)

Consequences should be clearly spelled out, and punitive action should be linked with counseling and treatment. Examples:

▶   meetings with parents

▶   contract signings (students sign contracts stating that they agree to abide by the rules)

▶   suspension, in-school suspension, and alternative schools

▶   referral to counselors

▶   notification of police

3. *Schools should implement security measures to eliminate alcohol and other drug problems.* Examples:

▶   student passes

▶   locker searches

▶   hall, restroom, and playground monitors

4. *Schools should distribute copies of their policy to all administrators, teachers, parents, and students and take steps to publicize it.* The policy can be incorporated into the school handbook(s).

5. *Schools should reach out to the PTA, police, and treatment organizations to work together.*

Last but not least, it's important for schools to provide training for teachers in awareness and prevention. Teachers who can't answer their students' questions may miss opportunities to discourage young people from experimenting or giving in to peer pressure. Teachers who joke about alcohol or drug use may send the wrong message to students. Even light comments such as "I've got a hangover" or "I need a drink to handle this class" are inappropriate and misleading.

8

Environmental Issues

▾▾▾▾▾▾▾▾▾▾▾▾▾▾▾▾▾▾▾▾▾▾▾▾▾▾▾▾▾▾▾▾▾▾▾

All of the environmental dangers that can affect people at home—including asbestos, lead, radon, and others—are also present in schools. But there are two major differences between environmental dangers in schools vs. homes. First, some problems are more prevalent in schools than in homes. Second, in some cases there are special laws that apply to schools concerning what to do about various problems.

As time goes on, there will most likely be more laws added and enforced pertaining to environmental issues. Meanwhile, schools are taking widely divergent approaches to environmental concerns. Some proactive schools are testing for and remedying situations before laws are passed. These smart schools know that there are legal and public relations reasons to go on the offensive today against environmental toxins, if only to avoid future lawsuits. But many schools, either because of lack of funds or lack of interest, regard environmental guidelines and recommendations as annoyances and don't do anything about them. Parents are in a unique position to change this inaction into action. Some parents might wonder, "Why should we try to get schools to address environmental problems that we haven't even investigated in our own homes?" School officials wonder the same thing. There are two good answers to this question:

1. *Schools serve hundreds of children in a community.* If an environmental toxin is present in a school, it is likely to hurt far more people than if it is present in a home.

2. *Schools are ideally positioned to set an example and play a leadership role in the community.* For example, when parents learn that schools are testing for lead in the drinking water, they might take the initiative to test their own water at home.

This chapter describes several environmental hazards that may or may not affect your child's school. If you suspect that the school might be affected, don't panic! Unless there is an acute emergency, get your school safety committee working on the problem, and remember that most of these dangers are long-term issues. The school should not rush to address a complaint before considering all available options. One reason to take a cautious, informed approach is the high cost of compliance.

Asbestos

Asbestos in schools became a national concern as recently as the fall of 1993, when New York City delayed the start of public school for one million students and spent $30 million to reinspect the schools and determine the extent of the asbestos problem. During this process, it was discovered that a program federally mandated in 1986 to find and remove damaged asbestos in schools not only had been poorly run but also had probably been fraudulently run. Schools still had huge amounts of "friable" asbestos (asbestos that crumbles easily when touched) that were releasing cancer-causing fibers into the air. In addition, it was found that poor or nonexistent maintenance had allowed problems like leaking roofs to go unrepaired, causing further damage to the asbestos in the schools' ceilings and walls.

Asbestos was one of the first environmental hazards to be identified in schools. It is generally agreed by the Environmental Protection Agency (EPA) that asbestos is present in most, if not all, school buildings in the United States. Although asbestos was known to be a health hazard in the 1970s, it wasn't until 1986 that Congress passed the Asbestos Hazard Emergency Response Act (AHERA) to protect students and staff from exposure to asbestos in schools.

Asbestos is a mineral which, when mined and processed, forms fibers too small to see. If these fibers are released into the air, they are so tiny and light that they stay in the air for hours, increasing the chances of inhalation. The fibers can cause lung cancer if inhaled over a long period of time—about ten years. AHERA outlines the steps that must be taken to make sure that asbestos is dealt with properly.

The EPA's Asbestos Ban and Phaseout regulation, issued in July of 1989, requires that asbestos be phased out of almost all uses by 1997.[1] Asbestos is used as insulation and in various building materials such as floor and ceiling tile, cement pipe, corrugated paper pipe wrap, acoustical and decorative insulation, pipe and boiler insulation, and spray-applied fireproofing.[2] It is only a problem when the fibers are released due to damage or deterioration. Friable asbestos is one type of "bad" asbestos. Asbestos becomes friable when it is damaged or deteriorates over time. Even "new" asbestos can become friable if damaged. Other asbestos products can release fibers when sanded, sawed, or removed. Materials containing asbestos in good condition pose little or no risk to people.

According to the EPA and AHERA, this is what your district should do about asbestos:[3]

1. Designate and train a person to oversee asbestos-related activities in the school system.

2. Inspect every school for friable and non-friable asbestos.

3. Prepare a plan for managing all asbestos and controlling exposure.

4. Consult with accredited inspection and management professionals about a plan to deal with the asbestos. Their responsibilities might include:

▶ maintenance to keep existing asbestos in good condition,

▶ repairing damaged insulation,

▶ encapsulating the asbestos,

▶ enclosing the asbestos, and/or

▶ removing it under special procedures.

5. Notify the public about the asbestos inspection and the availability of the plan for review.

6. Keep records of all asbestos-related activities.

Your parent safety committee can look into how your district is dealing with these requirements.

Air Pollution

Indoor air pollution in schools can cause staff and especially children to suffer from "sick building syndrome." If your child has a respiratory ailment, dizziness, or headache that only seems to occur at school, poor air quality is a possible cause.

A 1992 study done by the New York State United Teachers Union found that one in ten of the public schools in New York have internal air pollution.[4] There is good reason to assume that children in *any* school might suffer from this problem.

Air pollution can be present in old and new schools. In old schools, decayed particles are released into the air from walls and ceilings that may contain lead and asbestos. These particles are then spread around through heating and cooling vents. Newer schools with airtight construction and no windows trap gases from building materials. Indoor air pollution in schools will likely get worse as maintenance cutbacks eliminate or postpone the cleaning of heating and cooling ducts.

The New York State United Teachers study and other reports say to look for these symptoms of sick school building air:[5]

▸   soot-darkened areas around exhaust grills

▸   black or green growth anywhere (indications of microbial contamination from fungi, bacteria, and mold that thrive in warm, wet environments)

▸   dirty and/or wet carpeting (try to get it removed)

▸   excessive dust

▸   uneven temperatures throughout the building

▸   outdoor air contamination from garbage dumps, street traffic, or running school bus engines near windows or air intake vents (this causes carbon monoxide to enter the school)

▸ lingering odor(s)

▸ illness that disappears outside the building

▸ cigarette smoke (see pages 144–147).

In some cases, an easy solution is to open windows. (Sometimes windows need to be fixed before they can be opened.) In schools with few windows or windows that don't open, the ventilation system should be checked for any problems. Other solutions include testing for radon (see pages 151–152) or for carbon dioxide buildup (from respiration) in airtight buildings. You might ask the school nurse to keep a record of students with complaints that could be related to air pollution.

If you have more detailed questions about school air pollution, contact your State Department of Health and your state's division of occupational health.

Air Conditioning

In 1992, the Newark *Star-Ledger* was the scene of a lively letters-to-the-editor debate about air conditioning in schools. Over a period of weeks, many readers contributed opinions both pro and con. People feel very strongly about this issue!

Those who were *against* air conditioning in schools offered these arguments:

▸ Why should taxpayers fund air conditioning in schools when those at lower income levels can't afford it in their own homes?

▸ If teachers want air conditioning so badly, let them pay for it out of their own salary.

▸ We endured hot conditions in schools when we were growing up. We solved the problem by going outside and learning about nature.

▸ If the weather is too hot, schools should just close down for the day.

The arguments *for* air conditioning in schools included:

▸ All other public areas, like malls, theaters, and government buildings, have air conditioning, so schools should, too.

▸ Our society's lack of respect for education leads people to think that students, teachers, and administrators don't need air conditioning in order to function well.

- Most schools already have some air conditioning—in the administrative offices. Teachers, staff, and students shouldn't have to suffer through extreme heat. (Interestingly, it's often administrators who feel that there is no need to fund additional air conditioning.)

- Our society funds air conditioning for prisons, but not for schools.

- In an age when virtually every office and store has air conditioning, it doesn't seem extravagant to provide it to students and teachers.

I propose another compelling reason for schools to have air conditioning: the health and safety of everyone, including students, staff, and administrators. Specifically:

- Air conditioning can lessen or prevent violence. Comfortable people are less likely to get irritable.

- It's quite common for students to faint in school when temperatures become unbearable.

- Air conditioning can help alleviate air pollution.

If a school is considering year-round classes, or if it is already being used for summer extension programs, it *must* have air conditioning.

What can you do to get air conditioning in your child's school? You might start by asking for donations from businesses and individuals of new or used window units. If only a few units are available, good places to put them are rooms that are used by all students, such as the media center or computer room. (These need air conditioning anyway, to protect the equipment and keep it running.) You're on your own after that in deciding which classrooms should be first in line for any remaining units.

Of course, the optimal solution is funding from the district. Since this is uncharted territory, your best choice may be lobbying the school board directly.

Smoking

Maribel is listening to her health teacher talk about the hazards of smoking. Maribel knows the dangers personally; her grandmother had a heart attack at age 50, and the doctors said it was because she had smoked since she was a teen. After seeing the pain and fear her grandmother experienced, Maribel is convinced that she'll never smoke, even if her friends pressure her.

Then, after health class, outside school, Maribel sees her music teacher light up a cigarette.

What impression will this make on Maribel? Will she think, "This school is strange—one teacher tells me that smoking can kill you, while another teacher smokes right here at school"? Will she tell herself, "That teacher is really stupid"?" Will she be compassionate and think, "That music teacher needs some education on the health hazards of smoking"? Or will she wonder, "Who's right, the health teacher or the music teacher? Maybe smoking isn't so bad after all." Since many young people think they are immortal, this last conclusion is likely.

Whichever way Maribel views the situation, both the school and the students come out losers. Since most schools already include anti-smoking information in health lessons, they risk looking hypocritical if they do not also become smoke-free. In fact, many schools across the United States already are smoke-free, or tobacco-free. A totally tobacco-free school prohibits smoking in school buildings, on school grounds, or at school-sponsored activities. The policy applies equally to students, staff, and visitors.

Some schools and/or districts with no-smoking rules have less encompassing policies. For example, they may prohibit smoking anywhere by students and allow smoking by staff in the building or, as in Maribel's school, on the grounds. They might even allow students to smoke on the grounds if they are of legal age.

"It is inconsistent to teach tobacco prevention and cessation in schools and then provide designated smoking areas for students or staff. Let us not send confusing messages to our students!" says Connie Acott, director of the Colorado Tobacco-Free Schools and Communities Project, which has helped almost half of Colorado's schools become tobacco-free in four years.[6] If you want to look into establishing tobacco-free policies for your school, here are some additional facts and pointers to help you in your quest:

▶ The hazards of smoking are well-established in many reports available from your public library.

▶ A January 1993 report by the EPA concluded that environmental tobacco smoke, or ETS (the smoke emitted by the smoldering tip of a cigarette), when combined with smoke exhaled by smokers, is a group-A carcinogen.[7] Another report says that placing smokers and non-smokers in separate rooms that are on the same ventilation system probably will not eliminate exposure to ETS.[8] Therefore, if *anyone* is smoking in a school, student health is jeopardized.

▸ Total no-smoking environments have become the rule rather than the exception in our society. Cities, states, and businesses are creating no-smoking offices and restaurants.

▸ Common sense tells us that adults who smoke in and around schools are poor role models for impressionable students.

▸ Schools that allow students to smoke even on the grounds could be encouraging students to ignore laws that make it illegal for people under age 18 to purchase cigarettes.

▸ When the National School Boards Association conducted a 1988 nationwide survey of tobacco-free schools, they found excellent to good compliance with total smoking bans.[9]

▸ More and more states are passing legislation at the state level to ban smoking. These laws make it much easier for schools to comply.

A Legal Memorandum issued by the National Association of Secondary School Principals called "Smoking Policies: Implications for School Administrators" has information of interest to parents as well as principals.[10] In part, it discusses the pros and cons of smoking bans. On the one hand, "cigarettes are a legal product and, as adults, school personnel have the right as a matter of personal choice to decide whether to smoke." If smoking is banned, there may be employee dissatisfaction. On the other hand, "the school district's common-law duty is to provide employees with a safe workplace." (I would rephrase this as "employees *and students*.") Schools that don't ban smoking may be subject to lawsuits.

In general, the rights of people not to breathe smoke have found more support that the rights of people to smoke. The bottom line is: *Safe schools are smoke-free schools.*

According to the Colorado Tobacco-Free Schools and Communities Project, tobacco-free schools can be initiated by anyone, including parents. The steps it recommends are the same as those you would take for any other safe school initiative: commitment, committee, policy review and writing, school board approval, communication, implementation, and evaluation.[11]

The communication of a no-smoking policy is particularly important. Students, staff, parents, and community should know all of the reasons why the policy is in place. In addition, before implementing the policy, schools should decide what they are going to do with noncompliant people. For example, what about parents who come to pick up their children and smoke on the school lawn, even though the ban extends to the school grounds? Or what about the parent who smokes in the bleachers at a ball game, which is a fire hazard as well as a smoke hazard? A polite reminder of the rules is usually enough. "You are not trying to change everyone into nonsmokers," Connie Acott says. "You are merely identifying a behavior expectation."[12] What if a polite reminder of the rules isn't enough? Then you should protect your own health by changing your seat or location.

Of course, if you or your spouse is a smoker, you need to stop. Most children pick up the habit of smoking from a parent. Chewing tobacco and snuff are killers as well and should not be allowed. Talk to your children about how to resist pressure from peers to use tobacco products. An excellent resource for teaching these skills is *Peer Pressure Reversal* by Sharon Scott (see page 132).

Lead

Those convenient little water fountains that dot the halls of every school may be spouting water that is tainted with lead. Parents' reaction to this realization can range from "What's all the fuss about?" to "This is a serious problem!"

The presence of lead in our schools is one instance where a small amount of hysteria may be appropriate. Lead is a toxic metal and an unseen danger that even at low levels of exposure has been proved to cause nervous system damage, learning disabilities, and impaired growth and hearing. Worst-case scenarios can result in coma and kidney and brain damage. When we add to these concerns the fact that lead poisoning may present either no symptoms or symptoms that are nonspecific to lead, such as headaches and irritability, we begin to see the extent of the problem.

Lead affects children more than adults. Their bodies absorb more than adults', and when they play they come into closer contact with it. Therefore, parents should be particularly concerned about checking into all possible sources of lead exposure in schools. The two most common sources are:

▸   the drinking water, and

▸   paint chips and dust, which children inadvertently ingest when they get
them on their fingers.

In some cases, soil around the school can be contaminated from old paint that
was scraped off before repainting and not properly disposed of.

If you think that your child has been exposed to lead, ask your pediatrician
to arrange for lead testing. There are new treatments available to help children
who are affected by lead poisoning.

Lead in School Drinking Water

Two federal laws specify how the problem of lead in school drinking water
must be addressed. Importantly, neither law actually *requires* testing for lead.

1.   The Safe Drinking Water Act Amendments of 1986 require the use of lead-
free pipe and solder in the installation and repair of any public water system.

"Lead-free" is not a totally accurate term, however. Like "caffeine-free"
soda, which contains traces of caffeine, "lead-free" pipes and solder are allowed
to contain 8.0 and 0.2 percent lead, respectively. And even though states were
required to adopt this ban by June of 1988, a government spokesperson (who
asked not to be identified) acknowledges the possibility that it is not being
enforced.

2.   The Lead Contamination Control Act of 1988 requires the EPA to provide
guidance and grants to states to test for and remedy lead contamination in
drinking water in schools. However, according to the government
spokesperson, the EPA *authorized* $90 million for this purpose but never
actually *appropriated* any money. Even if laws are eventually passed that require
mandatory testing, there are not enough testing facilities or funds to deal with
the enormity of the problem.

How does lead get into drinking water? It leaches in from lead pipe
corrosion, solder, fixtures, or other parts of a plumbing system, in schools
both old and new. Elevated lead concentrations in school drinking water are
found most often when school resumes after vacations or weekends, because
the water has been sitting in the pipes absorbing whatever lead is present there.

This is one reason why lead in school water is a greater risk to children
than lead in the home. At home, water is used during weekends and vacations,
and lead is regularly flushed out. To be on the safe side, you should run the

water for a few minutes even at home to flush out water from plumbing that hasn't been used for more than six hours.

Schools can also use flushing as a remedy. This method has been criticized because it is wasteful, but it is much less expensive than other remedies including corrosion control, special filters, replacement of parts, or purchased bottled water dispensed from coolers. In fact, the high cost of removing lead from school drinking water has resulted in many schools failing to comply with lead testing recommendations.

A November 1991 article in *The American School Board Journal* explored some of the reasons why testing has been neglected.[13] The article reported that it was impossible for school districts to get the funds appropriated to them for testing, and since testing wasn't mandatory, it was a "back-burner" issue. A spokesperson for the EPA was quoted as saying, "The situation was that testing might have caused a lot of headaches for school administrators. And the tendency was not to deal with it." Another problem mentioned was that even if testing was done, it often involved only one or two locations within a school—not enough.

For more information, call the EPA's toll-free safe drinking water hotline: 1-800-426-4791. Request the free booklets "Lead in School Drinking Water" and "Drinking Water Coolers That Are Not Lead Free." The latter lists model numbers of plumbing fixtures that are known to contain lead, although a disclaimer states that other models may also contain lead. In other words, the only way to know for sure is to test the water.

▼ ▼

WHAT YOU CAN DO ABOUT LEAD
IN SCHOOL DRINKING WATER

1. Start by approaching the principal. Ask if the water at your child's school has been tested yet for lead.

2. If the water has been tested, ask to see the test results. Don't be surprised if you are referred to another person in the district; it's possible that your school doesn't keep the test results on site.

Who is in charge of testing a school's water for lead? That depends. If it's not the principal, it might be the superintendent, the head of the building facilities department, the science department head, or an outside tester hired by the district. In fact, this variety of responsibility is one of the main problems with how lead is handled. It's hardly appropriate to burden science teachers or principals with environmental safety when that is not their job nor their training. Nor are these individuals impartial, even if proficient.

3. If the water has not been tested, ask that it be tested as soon as possible. Ideally, each fountain and water faucet should be tested, because pipes can differ from location to location.

The cost of testing should be paid by the district; testing a sample from each location costs up to $30. The entire plumbing system should also be analyzed.

Many environmental advocates believe that there should be a federal superfund to pay for all lead testing. In the meantime, if money is absolutely not available, this could be funded by a parent group.

If testing at a particular location finds a lead concentration over the limit, the EPA recommends taking that location out of service until a remedy can be found. The EPA's recommended allowable limit is 20ppb.

4. Meanwhile, tell your child to let the water run for a few minutes before drinking at a school fountain. Or you might consider supplying your child with small containers of bottled water to drink from at school. Make this fun and easy for your child by giving him or her a personal water bottle holder. These are generally made of webbed nylon or leather straps. The bottom straps hold the water bottle, and the top strap can be worn over the shoulder for hands-free carrying.

▼ ▼

Lead in School Paint

When it comes to lead poisoning from paint, experts agree that children are at greater risk at home than they are at school. However, dust from old, peeling leaded paint is a definite health hazard. So is paint dust caused by renovations. In addition, any exposure at home is compounded by exposure at school.

A lead-in-the-paint problem costs even more to remedy than a lead-in-the-water problem. Removing lead paint is also more dangerous. In addition, no regulations exist for lead paint removal, nor is any certification required.

If you notice that renovations or inadequate maintenance practices are causing a lot of dust around your child's school, ask that the dust be tested for lead.

Radon

The conditions for this odorless, colorless gas exist underground in over 30 states, and radon is just as likely to contaminate schools as homes. In fact, the EPA announced in March 1993 that more than 70,000 classrooms in the United States and nearly one out of every five schools has unacceptably high levels of radioactive radon gas.[14] This announcement led Representative Henry Waxman (D–California) to observe, "It may be more dangerous to attend school than it would be to work in a nuclear power plant."[15]

This is probably an exaggeration. Experts say that because of the way schools are constructed, radon is less of a problem there than in homes. However, there is still cause for concern.

Radon gas is formed by the decay of uranium in shale rock and other soil elements. As this natural breakdown occurs, the gas seeps into buildings through cracks and clings to dust particles. When these particles are inhaled, they release radiation into the body and damage lung tissue. Prolonged exposure (10 to 30 years) can lead to lung cancer.

Fortunately, radon quickly dissipates in fresh air. So if your child's school or classroom is well ventilated, there probably is no need to be overly concerned. But if your child's classroom is in a basement or a room with windows that are always closed, you might want to look into whether the school has been tested for radon.

If the school decides to test for radon, each room should be tested individually, since radon levels can vary widely from one room to another and even from season to season. The testing is usually done with one of two devices: the charcoal canister or the alpha-track detector. The measurements are reported either in picocuries per liter (pCi/L, a radiation unit named after physicist Madame Curie) or as working levels (WLs). A reading of 4 picocuries is considered the maximum acceptable level of exposure. WLs are multiplied by

200 to estimate the amount of radon. For example, 0.02 WL is approximately 4 pCi/L.[16]

Correcting radon problems is easier than correcting for lead or asbestos. Often, it simply means opening windows more frequently or fixing stuck windows so they do open. Low-level radon can be eliminated by sealing foundation cracks. Sometimes a procedure called sub-slab ventilation is done on schools. A pipe is run from the slab floor up to the roof, and a fan is put on the pipe to suck out the radon from the ground and release it outside through the roof.

Dave Mizenko, a research scientist for the New Jersey State Radon Program, suggests that interested parents contact their regional or state EPA office to find out if their school was built on land with a radon problem.[17] This easy step can calm any fears, especially if the answer reveals no radon problem in your area. If there is radon in your area, ask the school to test for it if it hasn't already, and ask the school board about abatement plans. The Indoor Radon Abatement Act of 1988 can possibly provide grants.

For more information, call the toll-free National Radon Hotline at 1-800-SOS-RADON (1-800-767-7236).

Pesticides

If you have ants in your kitchen and dandelions on your lawn, do you spray them with insecticides and pesticides? Or do you follow more environmentally friendly methods? Perhaps you use natural insect repellents or pull up the dandelions by the roots and add them to your compost pile.

Most schools react to pests—cockroaches, weeds, rodents—with large-scale chemical warfare. Citing "health code regulations," they regularly spray all kinds of pesticides in and around schools without regard to whether the previous dose eliminated the pest or how student and staff health might be affected. According to *Public Citizen*, the publication of the research, lobbying, and litigation organization founded by citizen advocate Ralph Nader, "It is the school district's choice to interpret the health code as an order to spray pesticides: school officials could employ integrated pest management (IPM) techniques and enjoy pest and pesticide free kitchens and lawns."[18]

Integrated pest management seeks to control pests by using less chemicals. According to the EPA, IPM "is the coordinated use of pest and environmental information with available pest control methods to prevent unacceptable levels of pest damage by the most economical means, and with the least possible hazard to people, property and the environment.... Because IPM programs apply a holistic approach to pest management decision making, they take advantage of all appropriate pest management options, including, but not limited to pesticides."[19] Instead of spraying chemicals on a regular timetable regardless of pest population(s), IPM monitors and evaluates each site before applying chemicals. Options besides chemicals are considered. Depending on the pest, levels above zero may be allowed if there is no risk to people.

In general, most schools don't want to change their pest control methods because the current ones work and because other things seem more important. In addition, IPM is harder to use because it requires additional information and is site specific. However, like other new approaches to old problems, IPM is worth looking into.

Why all this concern about limiting the use of chemical pesticides? Because students and staff are being hurt from inhaling fumes and ingesting powders; because children's behaviors tend to expose them to higher levels of chemicals when they are around. For example, *The Journal of Pesticide Reform* reported that a boy in the state of Washington was poisoned by a pesticide that looked like "sand." The pesticide was placed on maple trees on the school grounds. The first grader tasted the "sand," vomited and fainted a few hours later at home, and nearly died. According to the *Journal*, there have been many other incidents like this at schools.[20] To complicate the problem, many symptoms of pesticide exposure (itchy eyes and throat, nausea, dizziness) may go undetected and untreated because they resemble symptoms of other childhood illnesses and allergies.

▼ ▽ ▼ ▽ ▼ ▽ ▼ ▽ ▼ ▽ ▼ ▽ ▼ ▽ ▼ ▽ ▼ ▽ ▼ ▽ ▼ ▽ ▼ ▽ ▼ ▽ ▼ ▽ ▼ ▽ ▼ ▽ ▼

WHAT YOU CAN DO ABOUT PESTICIDE REFORM

If you want to look into pesticide reform in your child's school, you might start by asking these questions suggested by the Northwest Coalition for Alternatives to Pesticides and the EPA:[21]

1.   Which pests are present?

2.   What pest control methods are currently being used?

3.   How often are they used?

4.   Are parents and teachers given advance notice that these methods will be used? (This is very important. If it is not being done, initiate this procedure as soon as possible. Ask to be notified.)

5.   Who makes the decision about whether to use pesticides?

6.   Are nontoxic alternatives considered?

7.   Does the school only hire licensed applicators? (These are professionals specially trained to apply pesticides.)

8.   What are the names of the chemicals being used?

9.   How do they work?

Once you learn which pesticides are being used, call the EPA's toll-free pesticide hotline: 1-800-858-7378. Find out as much as you can about the chemicals including toxicity, symptoms of exposure, and how to minimize risk.

For information about other options, write or call the Northwest Coalition for Alternatives to Pesticides:

- NCAP
  P.O. Box 1393
  Eugene, Oregon 97440
  Telephone: (503) 344-5044

▼ ▽ ▼ ▽ ▼ ▽ ▼ ▽ ▼ ▽ ▼ ▽ ▼ ▽ ▼ ▽ ▼ ▽ ▼ ▽ ▼ ▽ ▼ ▽ ▼ ▽ ▼ ▽ ▼ ▽ ▼ ▽ ▼

EMFs

EMFs—Electromagnetic Fields—are the newest environmental concern in communities and schools. While there has been evidence since the 1970s that magnetic fields emanating from power lines and other sources were related to higher than normal cancer rates, especially leukemia in children, not much has been done to study them.

As Paul Brodeur points out in his book, *Currents of Death,* "What may well delay the implementation of such badly needed research is fear among people in positions of authority and responsibility in the private sector, as well as in the state and federal governments, that if further investigation supports present indications that low-level electric and magnetic fields pose a health hazard, correcting the problem will prove to be not only tremendously expensive but also disruptive."[22] Brodeur notes that most public reports on EMFs have focused on the easily seen (and more easily remedied) high-voltage lines, not on local distribution wires, which are also a problem.

In any case, parents are starting to get angry that more studies have not been done and more effort has not been put into protecting our children. Many parents understandably feel that EMFs should be considered guilty until proven innocent, and that prudent avoidance measures (wisely and cautiously avoiding contact with EMFs) should be taken, especially concerning schools. Some states, like New Jersey, are starting to look into setting minimum exposure standards for schools. California has already adopted guidelines. Sweden has adopted rules as well.

▼ ▼

WHAT YOU CAN DO ABOUT EMFS

What can parents do about EMFs in schools until scientists and the government find out exactly how they affect our bodies and those of our children? If your school has high electric towers looming over it, chances are that someone in your state is already looking into the readings. If there are no towers nearby, EMFs may still be present from inside wiring, lighting, and other electrical equipment.

1. Ask your principal and your school board what is being done about measuring EMFs. If the answer is "nothing yet," request that readings be taken.

If high readings are found in certain areas in and around the school, those areas should not be used, whether they are specific classrooms or certain parts of the playground.

2. Find out about computers and EMFs. For a detailed explanation of how computers manufactured before 1983 may emit EMFs, ask your PTA president for the April 1992 issue of *PTA Today*. Look for the article, "Are Computers Dangerous to Children's Health?," by Norma Miller.

3. Meanwhile, at home, minimize close exposure to EMFs. Electric blankets and home appliances like blow dryers, shavers, clock radios, televisions, and vacuum cleaners are all possible sources of EMFs.

▼ ▼

Other Environmental Concerns

There are other environmental problems that can exist at schools, but they are not as widespread as the ones already described in this chapter. You may wish to ask your district if any of the following have been identified as problems in your child's school:

▶ *PCBs.* These chemicals were banned in 1979. Found in electrical equipment, they are a suspected human carcinogen.

▶ *Ground contamination.* Land around schools can be contaminated with lead, arsenic, asbestos, sludge from prior dumping, and other toxic wastes and substances.

▶ *Underground storage tanks.* These are regulated by the Resource Conservation and Recovery Act of 1984 and must meet requirements concerning correct installation, spill and overfill prevention, and leak detection.

Your Right to Know

The Federal Emergency Planning and Community Right-to-Know Act of 1986 requires states to oversee workplace reporting of hazardous substances. Right-to-Know laws require schools and businesses to label all chemical containers on site, provide training to employees on how to deal with hazardous substances, and complete a survey of hazardous chemicals used in public facilities. Material Safety Data Sheets, which contain information on the properties of various chemicals and how they affect health, should be available at all schools. If they aren't available at your school, contact your Local Emergency Planning Committee (LEPC) or State Emergency Response Commission (SERC) and request copies. Call information for the telephone numbers.

Because of the large amount of work that compliance with Right-to-Know laws requires, schools grumble about having to do a lot of labeling and training. They also claim that no one ever looks at or cares about any of this information.

The Right-to-Know laws *do* help citizens, especially in times of emergency. For example, during a fire or explosion, the information required by the laws helps emergency workers to know what they are dealing with. The laws allow interested parents to look at and suggest alternatives to toxic cleaning fluids used in schools. They require science teachers to adequately store materials, and custodians to use materials properly. They have forced schools and other institutions to clean and organize their chemical storerooms and to discard—safely—any old substances that were sitting around. These laws can save lives.

Help your school officials feel that their hard work is not in vain. Exercise your right to know and ask to see the school's Material Data Sheets. For more information, call the Emergency Planning and Community Right-to-Know Information Hotline toll-free at 1-800-535-0202. Or write to the Environmental Protection Agency at:

- OS-120
  U.S. EPA
  Washington, DC 20460

▼ ▼

FIND OUT MORE

For more information about environmental problems in schools, contact the Environmental Protection Agency. Write or call:

- USEPA Public Information Center
  Mail Code 3404
  401 M Street, S.W.
  Washington, DC 20460
  Telephone: (202) 260-7751

Ask for a copy of the EPA's excellent free booklet, "Environmental Hazards in Your School."

▼ ▼

9

From Classroom to Cafeteria

▼ ▼

*I*nteractive and hands-on classes like science, art, and physical education make learning fun, but teachers must use extra caution to avoid accidents and injuries. Dangerous chemicals for science experiments, glues and markers with toxic vapors for art projects, and the lack of safety equipment for sports are just a few examples of what parents can be alert for. Also included here is a discussion of cafeteria safety.

Safety in the Science Lab

A student is stabbed by a classmate during horseplay when the teacher leaves a high school horticulture class unattended. The student is stabbed by an implement being used to study plants. A nine-year-old attending a summer program suffers burns over 25 percent of his body when chemicals he is using to make "sparklers" explode. A high school student is burned on her thigh by dry crystals of a dangerously caustic compound that causes permanent disfigurement. She sues the school—and loses.

These and other true horror stories from school science labs around the country highlight the need for diligent safety measures. In fact, more students are hurt by lab chemicals in school than in chemical companies because there is less emphasis on safety in schools. Chemical companies work with strict safety guidelines, and schools should, too. Balancing hands-on learning with safety is a constant challenge for science teachers, but it is one that can and must be met.

According to Dr. James Kaufman, director of the Lab Safety Workshop at Curry College in Milton, Massachusetts, fewer than five percent of the teachers he trains have planned what to do in an emergency or have written emergency plans. Other teachers have told him that they try to enforce strict safety rules but the principal says "don't bother."[1] The safest teachers provide constant supervision and issue both verbal and written instructions regarding hazards. They consider safety so important that they test for it on quizzes, not just offer it as enrichment.

Science experiments, especially those involving chemicals, can be dangerous, so teachers often shy away from them. However, some go overboard with dramatic demonstrations that can place students in physical danger. Teachers need to ask themselves if they really must allow kids to handle explosive chemicals, or is there another way to teach the same lesson?

Everyone should wear lab coats and goggles in all lab areas. Most states have laws mandating eye goggle use. For example, New Jersey's law states: "The board of education of every school district shall require each pupil and teacher in the public schools of the district to wear industrial quality eye protective devices while attending classes in vocational or industrial art shops or laboratories in which caustic or explosive chemicals, hot liquids or solids, hot molten metals, or explosives are used or in which welding of any type or any similar dangerous process is taught, exposure to which might have a tendency to cause damage to the eyes. Visitors to such classrooms or laboratories shall also be required to wear such protective devices."[2] Goggles should be American National Standards Institute (ANSI) approved. Goggles that are shared should be disinfected after each use in disinfecting solutions or ultraviolet cabinets and cleaned with soap and water on a regular basis.

The following safety equipment should also be available in school science labs: fire blankets, chemical spill neutralizers, gloves, and first aid equipment. There should be a broken glass disposal area and an eye wash area.

Cramped, overcrowded labs are unsafe labs. The National Science Teachers' Association (NSTA) says that science labs should be limited to 24 students, with a minimum of 1 square meter of lab space per student.[3]

Science fair projects done at home should be monitored by the teacher as well as the parent. Never let your child work on a science fair project alone, and only permit those experiments which have been pre-approved. According to Dr. Kaufman, "this means that the health and safety consequences of new experiments are thoroughly reviewed and discussed before the experiment is conducted."[4] Why? Among other reasons, students might get the idea to combine chemicals to "see what happens" and cause an explosion.

For more information about science lab safety, write or call:

⬤ Laboratory Safety Workshop
Curry College
Milton, MA 02186
Telephone: (617) 333-0500, extension 2220

▼ ▼

SEVEN WAYS TO GET INVOLVED IN SCIENCE LAB SAFETY

1. Ask to see a copy of the lab safety rules. If the school is practicing good public relations, they should distribute these to parents without being asked, but you may have to go in search of them.

2. Find out if there is a student safety contract. This form, signed by students, acknowledges that they've read the safety rules. Some contracts also include space for students to list and describe any medical problems.

3. Talk with your children about lab safety. Find out how they feel about the rules and whether they are willing to follow them. They may tell you that they don't want to wear goggles and lab coats. (Students often try to get out of wearing goggles even when the teacher is strict about enforcing their use.) Calmly discuss with your children the real danger of eye injury and skin injury from chemical contact.

If your children wear contact lenses, you should be aware that these can "wick" vapors and liquids into the eyes and also interfere with first-aid flushing in case of an accident. The National Society to Prevent Blindness has an advisory committee on industrial eye health and safety that has issued statements on contact lens wearing that lab participants should know about. For more information, call toll-free: 1-800-221-3004.

Science teachers often keep detailed accident report logs to protect themselves against liability. The more you talk with your children about lab safety, and the more you encourage them to follow the rules, the less chance there is that they will cause an accident—and be held responsible for it.

4. Talk with the teacher about lab safety. Ask specific questions:

▸ Has the teacher been trained in lab safety, first aid, and CPR? Is the training up-to-date?

▸ Is the room properly ventilated? Some experiments release toxic fumes.

▸ Are chemicals properly stored (especially flammable and volatile ones)? Are storerooms locked at all times?

▸ Is equipment properly maintained?

▸ Is there a telephone in the classroom? Are emergency numbers posted nearby?

▸ Are students required to wash their hands after lab?

5. Make sure that fire prevention is a priority. Request that the teacher arrange for a representative from the local fire department or a fire extinguisher manufacturer to visit the class and give a lesson on preventing and extinguishing lab fires.

6. Find out what the teacher would do if a serious accident occurred in the science lab. One good plan is for the teacher to call the office on the intercom and have someone there call for emergency medical help. Meanwhile, the teacher stays with the injured student(s) and administers first aid. Classes should be told ahead of time what to do if a classmate is injured, since the teacher will be occupied and won't be able to supervise them. Some schools find that emergency red hall passes are an effective tool. Students can grab one and run to the office for help. The red color alerts staff to an urgent situation.

7. Start a "booster club" for parents that addresses issues like fundraising for science lab safety, equipment purchases, and speakers. This suggestion comes from Dr. James Kaufman. Sports have boosters, so why shouldn't science?

▼ ▼

Safety in Art Class

After worrying about guns, knives, and drugs in schools, the possibility of hazardous art supplies in your child's school art class most likely pales in comparison. But although violent dangers may be more obvious, they are not alone in threatening deadly consequences. Hazardous materials such as rubber cement, permanent felt-tip markers, pottery glazes, enamels, spray fixatives, and wheat wallpaper paste are still being used by children, despite warnings about their toxic effects. Often, teachers and parents may not know about the hazards involved.

Children are at much greater risk than adults from toxic art materials. Both physiological and psychological factors place children at increased risk of developing a toxic reaction to chemicals in art materials. For example, children and teens have a more rapid metabolism than adults because they're still growing. This can result in faster absorption of toxic materials. Children are also at higher risk because of lower body weight. Psychological risk factors include the deliberate eating or mishandling of art materials.

What to Look for on Art Supplies Labels

In 1988, the Labeling of Hazardous Art Materials Act was passed, requiring warning labels on art materials with chronic hazards. This act amended the Federal Hazardous Substances Act to require chronic hazard labeling of art materials, and became effective in 1990. It requires that all chronically hazardous art materials carry a statement that such materials are inappropriate for children, and prohibits their purchase for children in grades 6 and below. Art materials that are labeled properly under this law must carry the statement

"Conforms to ASTM D-4236" or the equivalent. The Labeling of Hazardous Art Materials Act also preempted state laws on art materials labeling.

The Art and Crafts Materials Institute (ACMI) has developed and instituted a voluntary program that attempts to provide standards of safety in children's art materials. Products bearing their labels (AP for Approved Product, CP for Certified Product) have been "certified by an authority on toxicology associated with a leading university to contain no materials in sufficient quantities to be toxic or injurious to the body, even if ingested."[5] The ACMI HL seal refers to adult products.

Concerned teachers should choose materials labeled in conformance with the law ("Conforms to ASTM D-4236") and, as a secondary precaution, use CP/AP approved materials. Common sense is important, too. For instance, oil paint, while certified nontoxic, shouldn't be used by children because it requires the use of toxic solvents to thin and clean.

It is a common misconception that a product without any warnings on the label must be safe. If a product has no statement on the label at all, it means that it has not been analyzed to determine its toxicity. If you are confused by these labels, you are not alone.

Too Toxic for Children

According to the Center for Safety in the Arts, some of the most common toxic products mistakenly given to children to use in school are rubber cement, permanent felt-tip markers, and some clays and glazes. In most cases of use, teachers and school administrators are not even aware of the dangers these pose. Parents should make sure that their schools are not letting children under grade 7 use these, and older children should receive proper instructions as to their use and dangers.

The Center for Safety in the Arts recommends substitutions for these and other art products for children under age 12. Examples include:

▶ Instead of permanent markers that contain toxic solvents, use watercolor markers.

▶ Instead of rubber cements that contain toxic solvents and vapors, use white glue, school paste, glue sticks, or double-stick tape.

▶ Instead of powdered materials which can easily be inhaled, use premixed art materials only.

Contact the Center for Safety in the Arts for complete information on substitutions, and also for information on other school art health issues including examples of proper supervision, lead in oil paint and other supplies, solvents that can be fatal with one swallow, and more. Parents of junior and senior high school students can request information specific to them, as more advanced classes use more potentially hazardous materials. Teachers can order a poster, "Safer Substitutes in Art." Write or call:

- Center for Safety in the Arts
  5 Beekman Street
  New York, NY 10038
  Telephone: (212) 227-6220

Other Arts-Related Health Concerns

Sharing theatrical or commercial makeup for school plays and face-painting activities is a possible scenario for transmitting infections (*not* HIV, however). Parents can request individual sources of makeup or individual applicators.

If musical instruments are shared, especially those requiring mouth contact, transmission of infection is possible as well. Contact the Center for Safety in the Arts for information on cleaning and handling shared musical instruments, which includes using disinfectants approved by the Environmental Protection Agency (EPA).

Safety in Physical Education and Sports

Janet comes home from school complaining that she is always picked last for teams in gym class. Melissa whines that she has gym every day and wishes she didn't. Jeff's tooth got knocked out while playing soccer, and his parents are angry. Physical education and sports should be fun, so why all these problems?

Emotional Safety

Physical education experts are just beginning to understand the effects of physical education practices on the emotional well-being of students. In an effort to find out why so many children don't enjoy gym, they are discovering that it's not the fault of the children or the parents (although active parents often have active kids), but the nature of the way classes are run.

For example, take Janet's problem of always being picked last for teams. According to the National Association for Sport and Physical Education (NASPE), teams should not be chosen by student captains during class. Instead, they should be chosen by the teacher ahead of time in ways that "preserve the dignity of each child."[6]

Experts are suggesting more new ideas for improving students' emotional health in gym class. For example, some schools still require students to wear gym uniforms and take communal showers after class. Children's bodies are changing, and they are acutely aware of differences. Why not eliminate uniforms so they don't have to suffer the indignity of changing clothes in school? Also, why humiliate them by making them strip and shower in front of each other? It doesn't cost much to make showers private by installing partitions and hanging curtains.

NASPE also suggests keeping fitness testing and scores confidential, not using physical activity (laps or pushups) as punishment, keeping all physical education activities gender-neutral, and offering all activities equally to boys and girls. Maybe as these and other ideas are implemented, we'll have a nation of physically fit people instead of couch potatoes!

Activity Safety

Although Melissa complains about having gym every day, she actually is lucky when compared to children at most other schools in the United States. Physical education (PE) experts would like to see every child take gym this often; so far, only Illinois mandates daily PE, and the NASPE reports that eight states have no PE requirement at all.[7]

Even if your child has gym class frequently, however, this is no guarantee that he or she will be physically active in class. Much time is spent waiting or listening, not moving around. NASPE suggests that "continuous activity be planned for everyone." They also suggest that it be noncompetitive.[8]

While daily gym classes are a boon to fitness, some may be the scene of unsafe practices. For example, Michael Imber, professor of educational administration at the University of Kansas, notes that "the trampoline is the source of catastrophic injuries. If it is still part of the physical education curriculum in your school, you might want to change that. Children can get fit doing dancing and aerobics with no risk of catastrophic injury."[9] The sport of javelin throwing should also be eliminated due to its high injury factor.

Along the same lines, NASPE points out that some calisthenics, like jumping jacks and windmills, are "out of vogue" now because they place unnecessary stress on joints and muscles.[10] A better choice of exercises would be ones that keep the body in proper alignment. Check with your school physical education department about these.

Often, PE programs are designed for children with an intense interest in sports, rather than to improve children's general fitness. The NASPE would like to see more programs that "provide all children of all abilities and interests with a foundation of movement experiences that will eventually lead to active and healthy lifestyles."[11] In other words, it's not necessary to play a sport in order to get fit and stay fit.

Sports Safety

However, those children who do enjoy sports should be protected by the proper safety equipment. This is not always the case, as Jeff's parents discovered. Their son should have been wearing a mouth guard while playing soccer.

Whether your children participate in organized school sports programs or in extracurricular ones, be sure to check out the safety equipment situation. You may discover that such equipment is available but its use is optional, not mandatory. For example, there is much new safety equipment for baseball including softer balls, face protectors that attach to batting helmets, padded vests that prevent heart failure in the event that a student is hit by a hard ball, and safety bases, but none of these items are mandatory. Until they are, we can't really expect schools to supply them or students to use them.

Most schools require parents to sign permission slips before their children can participate in school sports programs. Most also offer insurance at special rates. If you choose to purchase insurance for your child, be sure to read the fine print. One family learned the hard way that such policies don't cover everything. When their son came home from football practice with a headache that quickly turned into severe pain and blurred vision, they rushed him to the hospital to discover that he had a concussion. The emergency room visit, X-rays, and CAT scan totaled a whopping $2,000. Shortly afterward, they received the bill, called the school, and learned that the policy they had purchased covered everything *but* football.

If your child is involved in a school sports program, take the time to find out the facts about the sport, its dangers, and risks. Check your local library or bookstore for books on sports safety. For more information, write or call:

- The National Youth Sports Foundation
  10 Meredith Circle
  Needham, MA 02192
  Telephone: (617) 449-2499

▼ ▼

LYME DISEASE ALERT

If gym class is held outdoors, teach your children to perform tick checks when they return home. This will help them to avoid contracting Lyme disease, which is carried by deer ticks.

▼ ▼

Cafeteria Health and Safety

All children should have a good, substantial breakfast before starting school. Nourishing food is a ticket to success in learning and lifelong health. Many schools provide free breakfasts to children whose families are not able to provide them, because the government realizes their importance as well.

For lunch, it's best to pack one at home—ideally one your child will eat instead of trading away or throwing in the trash. For new and interesting ideas, check out current cookbooks at your local library. If your child buys lunch at school, you can discuss together ahead of time which items he or she will buy. If the school offers too much junk food in vending machines, work with your parent group to encourage the school to replace these items with healthier ones. Schools should not sell candy, soda, potato chips, or high-fat pastry items in vending machines or in cafeteria lines.

The issue of nutritious food vs. junk food has a safety angle. Schools are under increasing pressure to provide less fried foods and more fresh fruits and vegetables. But many schools are claiming that kids aren't eating these foods when they are offered. In high schools with open campuses, students are leaving at lunchtime to buy fast food elsewhere. Since leaving the campus is unsafe, schools are opting to serve less nutritious foods so the students stay on campus. Rather than serve inferior food, why not close the campus? See pages 31–32.

According to American School Food Service Association publications, these are some of the most popular foods schools today are offering:[12]

- taco bars
- burritos
- burgers
- French fries
- pizza
- stuffed potatoes
- bagels
- frozen yogurt
- deli sandwiches
- salads
- egg rolls
- stir-fries
- pasta bars (similar to salad bars)
- milk shakes
- fruit juice
- bottled water
- low-fat ice cream

Not all of these items meet nutrition guidelines set by the National School Lunch Program. In addition, these guidelines are being challenged by nutrition and dietary experts. There is quite a bit of controversy over what constitutes an appropriate school lunch, and there probably won't be a clear resolution in the near future. In the meantime, it is up to parents to discuss lunches with their children.

Parents often complain to schools that kids don't have enough time to eat lunch and are rushed. This may be true, but it is a problem without an easy solution. If schools gave more time to lunch, they would have to take it away from learning—or extend the school day. It's better to provide children with food they like and can eat quickly than to battle the time issue.

Even though most kids have to eat lunch in school, schools don't want to feel as if they are running restaurants. They don't want to hear that your child isn't finishing her lunch, or that your child doesn't like the food available at school. If the school is offering basically healthful foods, it's up to you to work out the menu with your child. Schools are steadfast about this being the parent's responsibility, and they are probably right.

It is the school's responsibility to keep the cafeteria safe. This means regular department of health inspections and adequate supervision by adults who know CPR and the Heimlich Maneuver. Students must sit on chairs and eat at tables; they must not be allowed to play or walk while eating. Discipline in general must be as firm and fair as at other times during the school day.

10
Disaster Preparation

▼▼

No one likes to think about life-threatening disasters, especially when they concern our children at school. In fact, the odds are against anything terrible happening at school, and for that we can be thankful. But because schools take care of so many children, involve large and numerous buildings, and provide complex transportation and food service systems, they are natural sites for emergencies to occur without warning during school hours—and for those possibilities, we and our schools must be prepared.

Planning Ahead: The Emergency Policy

Most likely, there is a written emergency policy at the board of education regarding your school. Depending on what part of the country you live in, this policy should cover how the school will keep kids safe during an earthquake, hurricane, flood, wave action, tornado, lightning, hail storm, high wind, fire, landslide, explosion, chemical accident, bomb threat, animal in the school, bus or auto accident, structural collapse, electrical short, gas leak, hostage incident, terrorist attack, war, and more.

The policy should indicate the responsibilities of the principal, teachers, school nurse, and custodian during such emergencies. It should list community resources to call on for help and assistance—police, fire department, medical and rescue services. It should discuss first aid and evacuation procedures and spell out how kids will be kept safe until they can return home.

Will the school be used as a shelter by the community during an emergency? If so, the policy should indicate this and provide specific plans. Are students taught what they should know and do in the event of an emergency? This, too, should be covered by the policy. Call your board of education and request a copy.

Find out if your district has weather radios, which some schools have purchased as part of their disaster preparedness programs. The radios automatically click on if hurricanes or tornadoes hit the county. This gives schools adequate warning to prepare or evacuate. Weather radios might help to avert disasters such as the one that struck a Newburgh, New York, school in November 1989, where a cafeteria wall collapsed during a tornado and killed nine children.

When you study your district's emergency policy, you might notice something missing from it: any mention of parents. According to "Guidelines for Emergency Preparedness in Schools," a report from the Manitoba, Canada, Department of Education and Training, "It is important to involve parents in the school plan and to communicate the need for their support in its implementation.... The public relations benefits of the school emergency preparedness program are many. Parents will be relieved to know that plans exist to provide their children with the highest possible degree of protection.... Teachers will also find that in this, as well as in other school programs, parents can make a valuable contribution if they are kept informed."[1]

Even if parents know about and participate in emergency plans, there is still the possibility of uncertainty and confusion during an actual emergency. In its "Guidebook for Developing a School Earthquake Safety Program," the Federal Emergency Management Agency (FEMA) offers several excellent observations and suggestions that can be applied to *all* emergency planning:[2]

1. *Plan for the possibility that essential services and supplies—including water, gas, food, electricity, communications, and transportation—may not be available. Many*

emergency plans assume that these things will remain available and operative. But what if they aren't? In an earthquake, for example (which could happen almost anywhere), they may be severely disrupted. Parents might not be able to get to the school to help. FEMA suggests that parents near the school be organized into a network to supply the school with aid during an emergency.

2. *Find out which teachers have had training in first aid and CPR and publicize this fact.* School emergency plans usually assume that teachers will be able to perform first aid. In fact, most teachers are not trained in these or other emergency skills.

3. *Train children to understand and deal with many different types of emergency situations.* Most schools don't do this, claiming that "children will be frightened if they have to think about things like earthquakes (floods, tornadoes)." However, students everywhere are educated in fire safety. Fire is frightening, too, but most children would know what to do if one broke out at their school. It makes sense to teach them about other situations that require a fast response and an organized, orderly exit.

4. *Identify potential hazards in the neighborhood surrounding the school.* Parents can work together to identify manufacturers and users of toxic and radioactive materials (especially gas stations), railroads, major underground gas and oil pipelines, utility vaults and transformers, water towers, water tanks, and potentially dangerous buildings like those that are damaged or collapsed. Enlist the help of the fire department, city or county public works office, building inspection department, and the American Red Cross to find, warn about, and possibly remedy these dangers.

5. *If a disaster occurs in a school somewhere else, contact your school officials immediately afterward and initiate a disaster planning project.* Unfortunately, it is incidents like these that make people most receptive to the idea of taking action. You may not be able to help the other school, but you can take steps to ensure that your school is better prepared for a similar situation.

For more information about planning for emergencies, write to:

● Federal Emergency Management Agency (FEMA)
P.O. Box 70274
Washington, DC 20024

Request copies of "Guidebook for Developing a School Earthquake Safety Program" and "Are You Ready? Your Guide to Disaster Preparedness," which lists other organizations to contact for information on all sorts of emergencies.

Fires in Schools

A water heater explodes, killing six children and a teacher in Spencer, Oklahoma. Student arson in a trash can fills an Amesbury, Massachusetts, school with smoke. Student arson results in $200,000 worth of damage to a Texas school. In a high school in Michigan, a student and a teacher are burned in an auto shop fire. Stage lights ignite a curtain in a Florida high school. In Connecticut, a fire apparently caused by a duplicating machine that was accidentally left on destroys a school—a property loss in excess of $8 million.[3]

According to the National Fire Protection Association, there were approximately 9,000 fires in educational buildings in the United States in 1991—a 5.9 percent increase over 1990.[4] How do fires start in schools? Tridata Corporation, which supplies fire safety data to the federal government, has found that the main cause is arson.

Philip Schaenman, a fire safety consultant and Tridata's president, notes that in Japan every school child is taught the ethics of setting fires by the time they reach the third grade. In contrast, the *New York Times* reported in 1991 that "American fire departments are some of the world's fast and best equipped. They have to be. The United States has twice Japan's population, and 40 times as many fires. It spends far less on preventing fires than on fighting them."[5] The *Times* observed that in other countries, fires are treated either as personal failings or as crimes; in the United States, there is a widespread attitude that fires are not really anyone's fault. A 1990 ERIC report titled "Ignorance and Hazards in Academe: The Dilemma of Fire Safety in American Education" found a lack of interest in fire safety among college administrators.[6]

Parents must take more responsibility for teaching their children about fire, fire safety, and arson. Some curiosity about fire is normal; extreme curiosity or other unusual behaviors might indicate that a child has emotional problems that could lead to arson. Experts recommend that parents be alert to these clues:

▸ fire-starting materials (matches, lighters) hidden in the child's room

▸ suspicious fires in and outside of the home

▸ remains of fires (charred paper or garbage)

▸ small burns on furniture

▸ a too-intense interest in fires in general.

Children set fires to resolve tension, relieve aggressive feelings, show anger, and as a result of neglect. Any child who is found to have set a fire, no matter how small, should be brought to a mental health professional *at the very least*. If the trouble is repeated, the child should be enrolled in a community program aimed at juvenile fire setters.

After arson, which causes 43 percent of all school fires, Tridata lists the following reasons in descending order of frequency:[7]

- unknown
- electrical
- heating
- appliances
- open flame
- cooking
- careless smoking
- other equipment
- children playing
- natural causes
- other.

Flammable decorating materials and bulletin board materials can easily be ignited. A fire in a Halloween "haunted house" set up by parents in a Virginia elementary school killed one parent and injured two others.

Barriers to Fire Safety

A father was in a school cafeteria, helping his daughter get into her costume for a performance, when he noticed that the doors to the outside were chained shut. He asked a custodian to unlock them, fearing that the hundreds of children and parents inside might be prevented from exiting in case of a fire. The custodian unlocked the doors, but the father contacted the fire department a few days later to complain about the practice. This resulted in a newspaper report citing past problems at the high school regarding the same situation. Apparently the cafeteria doors were often chained at after-school programs and, in fact, the fire department had already ordered the high school to remove the chains and discontinue the practice.

Why had the principal continued to chain the doors against the orders of the fire department? The answer lies in one of the paradoxes of school safety today: The doors were chained to protect against vandalism. "What schools do for crime safety should not create a fire hazard," Philip Schaenman says.[8]

There are other common procedures that protect schools against vandalism and violence while conflicting with fire safety. Bars on windows keep glass from getting broken and prevent intruders; they also prevent students and staff from using the windows to escape from fires. Narrow checkpoints at building entrances facilitate weapons detection; they also prevent rapid evacuation in emergencies. Schaenman advises that barred windows have a "swing-away" feature so they can be opened from the inside. Also, checkpoints should be easy to dismantle.[9]

Political Problems

The principal who chained the cafeteria doors wasn't alone. Other school administrators have failed to cooperate when told to make changes in their fire safety practices.

A fire marshal concluded that the lunch room in an East Newark school was overcrowded; the kids were "sitting almost on top of each other." The lunch room was only supposed to hold 140 students; the school's population was 228, and there was only one lunch period. When the principal failed to comply with the fire marshal's request to add a lunch shift, the parents contacted the media.[10]

In another case, a principal disconnected the school's centralized fire alarm because there were "too many false alarms." When a fire actually did start in the school, there was much damage. It was later determined that the fire marshal had overlooked the dismantled alarm during inspections.

Some schools censor news about fires. One school newspaper wanted to publish a story about a small arson fire that had destroyed some bulletin boards. No one was hurt, but the halls smelled of smoke and the student editors wanted to report the story. The principal wouldn't let them.

I personally pulled my son out of a nursery school when I learned that the staff had censored information about a fire. The school had a smoke alarm system that was wired to the fire department. During a renovation, the workers disconnected the alarm system because the smoke from welding was setting it off. They forgot to reconnect it, and a fire started after hours from a smoldering ember. If a youth group hadn't smelled the smoke and called the fire department, the school would have been destroyed. Even though the school reeked of smoke, the staff denied to parents that there had been a fire. In a long private conversation with the director, I learned the truth—including the fact that fire exits were being blocked during the renovation.

"Grandfathered" Fire Codes

Fire safety codes get better and stronger every year, but because most of our nation's schools are older, they were built to lesser fire standards. All older buildings are "grandfathered," meaning that they are not required to bring their fire safety up to current code.

In addition, code enforcement is a relatively new profession. "Sixty years ago, many parts of the country didn't have a program to inspect and review school buildings," says Bob Brown, acting director of technical services for the National Conference of States on Building Codes and Standards.[11]

▼ ▼

SIX THINGS YOU CAN DO ABOUT FIRE SAFETY AT SCHOOL

1. Tell your children to act responsibly during fire drills and take them seriously. Tell them to stop what they're doing, listen for instructions, exit quickly, and stay out of the building until instructed to go back in. Everyone should know at least two ways out of the building.

2. Invite representatives from the fire department on a tour of the school. Arrange this with the principal in advance; the principal should also come on the tour.

As you walk through the school, look for the following fire hazards:

▶   exits that are entirely or partially blocked

▶   combustible materials stored under or in stairwells

▶   flammable material covering more than 20 percent of walls

▶   artwork and mobiles hanging from light fixtures

▸ student lockers stuffed with old papers and other combustible materials

▸ day care facilities that have hotplates and/or microwave ovens.

3. Ask for the dates of prior fire safety inspections. Ask whether any hazards were found and if they have been remedied.

4. Find out if false alarms are a problem. If they are, ask the school to do something about it.

False alarms waste schools' and firefighters' time and money, and they can divert firefighters from going to real fires. If students are pulling alarms as a "prank," a fire safety education program should be instituted. Making children aware of the dangers and the punishments involved—fines, imprisonment—should solve the problem. The NFPA has information on these kinds of educational programs; see #6 below.

5. Learn if the school has smoke alarms. If it does, find out where they are located and how they work. Ideally, the smoke detectors will be wired to the fire department.

Many schools don't have smoke detectors of any kind. Most don't have sprinkler systems. If your school is unprotected, join with your parent group to do something about it.

6. Ask your school to teach a fire safety curriculum. The National Fire Protection Association has information about fire safety curricula (and materials about home fire safety). To request a catalog, write or call:

● National Fire Protection Association
1 Batterymarch Park
P.O. Box 9101
Quincy, MA 02269-9101
Toll-free telephone: 1-800-344-3555

▾ ▾

11

Legal Issues

▼ ▼

Sam's son Ryan is in a wheelchair, and he can't get from the school building to the playground without being carried. Janice has decided to move her son to a different, safer school, but she'll have to lie and say that he's living with her sister. Thea is shocked to learn that a teacher at her daughter's school has just been arrested for dealing drugs. Elliott has been asking for months to have the drinking fountains at his children's school tested for lead, but nobody seems to be listening.

Each of these issues is covered by school law. Each of these individuals has legal recourse...or, in Janice's case, is taking a legal risk. School law is a powerful tool, and parents should have some knowledge of what it involves. School law is also enormously complex, so this chapter can't possibly go into great depth. Consider it an introduction to some of the issues that concern parents today.

The Americans with Disabilities Act

All parents should be aware of the rights of disabled students, not just those who have children with disabilities. These rights are outlined in the Americans with Disabilities Act (ADA) of 1990, which says that schools and other institutions may not discriminate against people with disabilities. The ADA not only addresses the needs of disabled students. It can also make schools safer for everyone. For example, levered doorknobs—which are a common request of disabled people—are easier to open than round ones, for both physically challenged students as well as all other children.

In 1993, the *New York Times* published an article titled "Wheelchair Warrior Lays Siege to Schools."[1] The article profiles a man who is an aggressive advocate for making schools accessible to persons with disabilities. It discusses how schools and school playgrounds must be accessible to children and adults with disabilities. It recaps what this can mean: ramps for entrances, accessible bathrooms, lowered water fountains, wider doorways, levered doorknobs, raised letter signs for the visually impaired, handicapped parking, elevators, and more. Any parent who is interested in talking to a school about renovations to make it accessible should read this article for a discussion of the costs and the issues involved. Ask the reference librarian at your local library to find it for you in the *New York Times Index*.

If you have a child with a disability, you might consider joining with other parents to form a Special Education PTA (SEPTA) to address the safety needs of your children. Start by calling your state or local PTA representative, or contact:

- National PTA
  700 North Rush Street
  Chicago, IL 60611-2571
  Telephone: (312) 787-0977

▼ ▼

RESOURCES FOR PARENTS OF CHILDREN WITH DISABILITIES

For specific (and free) safety information pertinent to children with disabilities:

- National Information Center for Children and Youth with Disabilities (NICHCY)
  P.O. Box 1492
  Washington, DC 20013
  Toll-free telephone: 1-800-695-0285

To find out more about how the ADA affects children's rights in school:

- Office on the Americans with Disabilities Act
  U.S. Department of Justice
  Civil Rights Division
  P.O. Box 66118
  Washington, DC 20035-6118
  Telephone: (202) 514-0301

▼ ▼

False Enrollment

Janice's son, Mark, spent a rough three years in the middle school in their district, and now Janice wants him to go to a high school where there aren't drug dealers and gang fights. She is considering enrolling Mark in the high school in the district where her sister lives. She's got it all planned: she'll enroll him using her sister's address, and if anyone asks, she'll say that they have moved in together. She'll drop Mark off at school on her way to work in the morning. In the afternoon, he can walk to her sister's house with her nephew, and she'll pick him up after work. Her sister will pass on to her any mail that the district sends to them. This way, the school will never know that she and Mark really live somewhere else, and Mark can go to school without fear of being mugged or shot at.

No one can fault parents for wanting their children to have the best and safest education possible, but Janice's idea is a bad one for two reasons. First, her son will be living with a lie. This will not only cause him great stress, it will also teach him that lying is acceptable. Second, false enrollment is actually a form of theft, with potential—and serious—legal consequences.

School districts are funded with local property taxes in the range of $3,000 to $10,000 per student per year. If a child attends a school in a district where his or her parents are not paying those taxes, that child (and his or her family) is effectively stealing that amount of money. Schools are becoming aware of this problem and are not looking the other way. They are hiring detectives to track down offenders and are expelling students who are illegally attending schools outside of their own district. The families are also being sued and billed for the cost to taxpayers.

Because of safety problems at many schools, more and more parents are considering or committing false enrollment. Educators are aware that some parents are:

▶ moving and not reporting they are living outside the district

▶ giving the address of friends or relatives

▶ faking a lease on a form bought at a stationery store

▶ installing a phone in someone's home to create the fiction of residency (one reason why schools no longer accept phone bills as proof of residency)

▶ claiming homelessness

▶ surrendering custody of their children to relatives near a desirable school

▶ renting rooms in someone else's home but not living there.

Of course, there are times when a student will reside with relatives for legitimate reasons. In cases like these, the school might ask the relatives to sign an affidavit saying that they are talking full responsibility for the student. If they are not willing to do this, the student is not allowed to register. In some cities, schools require residents who are raising other people's children to go to court and assume legal custody before the children can be enrolled in school.

In most districts, false enrollment is a disorderly conduct offense. This is a criminal offense punishable by a fine and/or imprisonment.

There are many ways students and families can be caught committing this crime. One of the saddest is when a young child proudly tells the teacher his or her phone number and address—in a different town. Sometimes detectives hired by the school ride buses and follow students to their true residences. Detectives also check license plate numbers and watch for cars with children that enter towns from main roads; parents have been known to cross state lines and major bridges to take their children to school in other districts. School attendance officers make surprise visits early in the morning or late at night to homes of students suspected of false enrollment. Some schools offer a bounty to citizens who report cases.

Unsafe schools are a tragedy, but false enrollment is not the answer. If you feel that you simply must move your child to a different school—if you have made your best efforts to teach your child about safety, if you have tried and failed to improve the situation—there are *legal* ways to switch schools:

▸ If your school is extremely overcrowded, it may be possible to obtain a variance (special permission) from the district for your child to attend another school.

▸ Some states allow students to attend school in any district in the state, subject to certain restrictions. Find out if your state is a "choice" state.

▸ Many public school districts offer out-of-district students a place in their schools if parents are willing to pay tuition.

▸ If all else fails and no other options are available, you may have to move to another district.

Teacher, Administrator, and Staff Crime

"The nuclear power industry and banks have access to criminal records. Why shouldn't we give kids the same protection?"

REPRESENTATIVE DON EDWARDS (D-CALIFORNIA)[2]

School staff crime is a hot safety issue around the country. Consider these headlines from newspapers in my area alone:

▸ "School Custodian Seized in Child Sex Abuse"

▸ "Irvington High Teacher Charged with Selling Cocaine to Student"

▸ "School Custodian Accused of Arson"

▸ "School Psychologist Is Charged With Sex Abuse"

▸ "Teacher Suspended Amid Molest Charges"

▸ "Teacher is Indicted in Fondling Incidents"

▸ "Teacher Gets Ten Years for Selling Drugs"

▸ "School Principal Charged in Marijuana Operation"

▸ "Girl Charges Sex Abuse by Teacher on Field Trip"

▸ "School Principal Arraigned on Abuse Charges"

What is going on here? How on earth is it possible that our educators are involved in these kinds of crimes? I don't pretend to have the answers, and no studies have as yet been done, but I can speculate. School staff members are human, after all, and crimes are committed by all sorts of humans. In addition, since sexual harassment and sex crimes in particular have become more reportable, it is only natural to see a reported increase. But there is more. There are issues here that have special bearing on schools and interest for parents.

Screening Measures

Experts have concluded that people with pedophile tendencies will naturally be attracted to the school setting as a place to work. In order to combat this, the American Bar Association Center on Children and the Law recommends that "screening measures must be sufficient enough to spot not only individuals with unintended dispositions toward abusive behavior, but also that small minority of people who willfully prey on youngsters assigned to their care and misrepresent their records and identification in order to do so."[3]

Of course, the overwhelming majority of school staff, teachers, and administrators respect and serve children in the pursuit of excellence in education. So how do bad ones sneak in? Through cracks in states' criminal history review statutes.

Since there is no national database that keeps track of school employee criminal records (although many people think there should be and are working to make it happen), it is hard for schools to do background checks on all job applicants. In addition, not all criminal records—including those for some forms of theft, blackmail, and income tax evasion—disqualify people from school jobs. And no matter how many times some people may have been arrested, they can't be disqualified from a job if they have never been convicted of a crime. In fact, if a school does come up with information about an arrest during a background check and wants to disqualify an applicant as a result, it must be careful not to break anti-discrimination laws. If a school refuses to hire an individual for this reason, it risks being sued for libel or slander. Yet if the school goes ahead and hires someone who turns out to be a problem, or waits awhile to investigate allegations, parents can rightfully charge negligence. Clearly, it is a serious problem when laws that protect the rights of employees directly affect the rights of children to have safe, qualified educators.

However, schools are realizing that they must be more careful about who they hire. Some resent the trouble and paperwork involved, while others are proactive and hire screening companies to check police records, motor vehicle bureaus, credit bureaus, educational records, and former employers. Many schools find that merely telling a potential applicant about this rigorous screening mechanism can discourage a person with an unsavory background from applying. While some private schools also have tough standards, others don't—one reason why private schools may not be any safer than public ones.

"What is happening is that in states with tough public school hiring laws, people that are prone to sex and drug problems are migrating into private schools," says Carl Caribelli, manager of the office of criminal history review in the New Jersey state department of education. Caribelli says that since 1987, he has disqualified over 1,800 school job applicants, 1,790 of whom lied on their applications.[4]

Substitute teachers are another potential problem area. Schools often have trouble finding acceptable substitutes, especially on short notice. Often, substitutes are allowed to teach before they have undergone background checks. In Fairfax City, Virginia, one substitute was found to be a convicted killer! Even when schools do background checks, they often take too long (months) and the school lets the employee work before getting the results. It has been suggested that this practice be discontinued and that employees only be allowed in schools after their background checks have been completed.

Parents should know that school personnel in all 50 states are required to reported suspected child abuse. The laws usually state that they must report the abuse within a certain amount of time, but they are not required to prove that the abuse occurred. This includes children that the teacher suspects are being abused by their parents, other students, or school personnel. For more information on child abuse, see pages 125–126.

What You Can Do

At the very least, you have a right to know exactly what your state does and does not require for school employee background checks. Call your state department of education to find out.

Call your legislators and encourage them to hold public hearings on this issue. Ask them why random drug testing isn't allowed for school employees when it is allowed for airline workers and police officers. Ask why Hawaii is the only state that requires fingerprint checks for all employees, and why more states—namely yours—do not require this. Meanwhile, be aware that there is no legal way for a parent to check on the criminal background of an individual teacher.

The School Board and School Law

"Anything parents can do to make their voices heard will help, from attending school board meetings to becoming active in the PTA to approaching teachers with questions or concerns."

DR. BENJAMIN SPOCK[5]

Suppose that you have a legitimate complaint about school safety (or any other subject). Communicating with the parents' organization, the principal, and the superintendent is not getting you anywhere. What's the next step? Bring your issue to the school board.

In most towns, this is an excellent way to get action taken, and it's reasonably easy to do: Call the board of education to find out when the next scheduled meeting is, attend, and present your ideas in an organized, calm, polite way. Most likely you will be received well and your issue will be discussed and acted upon.

There are exceptions, however. The National Committee for Citizens in Education (NCCE) warns that sometimes justice is not served even at this level. People may find that they are barred from meetings, meetings are not publicized, or too much red tape is required to get permission to speak. These obstructions of justice violate open meeting laws that every state has passed— "sunshine" laws that spell out citizens' rights to access school boards and other public bodies.

NCCE has published a book, *Beyond the Open Door,* that addresses the laws and requirements of each state regarding school board access.[6] It's a necessary first step to finding out how your state operates. To obtain a copy, write or call:

● National Committee for Citizens in Education
  900 2nd Street, N.E., Suite 8
  Washington, DC 20002
  Telephone: (202) 408-0447

The best way to find out more about how your local schools are run is to attend school board meetings regularly. The general public *should* be made to feel very welcome. You might even decide to seek a place on the board. If you do, you'll want to read *How to Run a School Board Campaign and Win*, also published by the NCCE.

If All Else Fails...

If you have brought your issue to the school board and it is still being given short shrift, there are two more options available to you: You can contact the media, or you can take legal action.

If you decide to contact the media, spend time in advance gathering your thoughts and preparing the materials that pertain to your issue. Try to anticipate questions that reporters may ask you—about specific incidents, people, your attempts to resolve the problem, and the like—and have your answers ready. You might even want to write them down and type them up so they look professional. You will want to present yourself as a serious, responsible parent with a legitimate complaint who has tried to find a solution by going through the regular channels. You are contacting the media as a last resort because nothing else has worked and the problem is too important to be dismissed.

The media—and the public—want to hear about school safety problems. Your efforts may lead to headlines that will focus attention on your cause. School boards don't enjoy being in the spotlight for negative reasons, and you may find that they are willing to listen and act quickly.

Start by calling your local newspaper and ask to speak to the city editor. If the editor thinks that your story is newsworthy—and it will be, if you have followed the suggestions outlined here—then a reporter will be assigned to look into the situation. Once you have called one newspaper, wait to see the results before you call another.

Bigger stories might interest television stations. If you decide to contact one, call and ask to speak to the assignment desk at your local station's newsroom. Again, if they are interested in pursuing the story, they will send a news crew out to talk to the people involved.

Taking legal action—suing the school—should be your last resort. Suing is costly in terms of time, money, and emotions, and it is not always satisfactory. Parents can win lawsuits, but they can also lose them.

Legal action is often taken in cases where a child is hurt in school. The National Committee for Citizens in Education advises that for parents to hold a school or its employees liable for injuring a student, they must be able to prove the following:[7]

1. There was a breach of duty and reasonable care.

2. The breach of duty was the cause of injury.

3. There was no contributory negligence.

These are all legal terms with specific legal meanings. For more information, contact the NCCE at the address and telephone number given above and request a copy of the book, *Parents, Schools, and the Law*. At the time of this writing, the cost is $10.50.

For examples of real cases where parents have taken schools to court, look for the periodical *Legal Notes for Education* at a nearby law library or education library on a college campus. (You can, if you wish, contact the publisher: Data Research, 1-800-365-4900. Be aware that this periodical is expensive.) You'll see that many cases brought by parents don't win because they don't meet the criteria outlined above. Another reason lawsuits by parents often fail is because the parents invest so much emotion in them that they won't settle even when it becomes clear that they can't win.

Obviously it is in the best interests of everyone—parents, school staff and teachers, and especially our children—to remedy any safety problems *before* they occur. Given the choice between headlines, settlements, and safe schools, we would all prefer safe schools. Let's work together to make that our goal.

Notes

Chapter One: Unsafe at School

1. Goodman, Ellen, "Mothers Can't Stave Off the World Forever," syndicated column, Newark *Star-Ledger*, May 8, 1992.

2. "Estimates Report: All Products—Injuries at School—Calendar Year 1992," U.S. Consumer Product Safety Commission, Directorate for Epidemiology, National Injury Information Clearinghouse, Rundate 6/15/93. Source: National Electronic Injury Surveillance System.

3. Karter, Michael J., Jr., "NFPA Reports on U.S. Fire Loss—1991," *NFPA Journal*, September/October 1992.

4. "School Crime, A National Crime Victimization Survey Report," U.S. Department of Justice, September 1991.

5. Telephone interviews with George Butterfield, Deputy Director, National School Safety Center, August 2, 1993, and January 4, 1994.

6. *A Survey of Experiences, Perceptions, and Apprehensions about Guns among Young People in America*, prepared for The Harvard School of Public Health, conducted by LH Research, Inc. in July 1993.

7. "Study Finds School Violence Strikes 23% of Students, 11% of Teachers," Newark *Star Ledger*, December 17, 1993, Metropolitan Life Survey of the American Teacher.

8. Telephone interview with Peter Blauvelt, school safety expert with the National Association of Elementary School Principals, director of Prince George's County Public Schools Department of Security Services, and chairman of the board of the National Association of School Safety & Law Enforcement Officers, August 6, 1993.

9. Berla, Nancy, "Getting Middle School Parents Involved," *ERIC Review*, September 1991.

10. Maze, Jerry, "The School District's Liability in Cases of Violent Attacks on Students and Employees," ERIC position paper, July 1991.

11. Million, June, "Principals Find Parents Eager for Advice on Education," *NAESP News*, May 4, 1992.

12. Fernandez, Joseph, with John Underwood, *Tales Out of School* (New York: Little, Brown, 1993), p. 264.

13. Telephone interview with Peter Blauvelt, August 6, 1993.

14. "President Clinton's Plan for Education," *Education Digest*, January 1993, condensed and reprinted from *Phi Delta Kappan*, October 1992.

15. Verhovek, Sam, "Texans Reject Sharing School Wealth," *New York Times*, May 3, 1993.

16. Braun, Robert, "The Monied Path Is a Dead End to Better Schools," education column, Newark *Star-Ledger*.

17. McKinley, James Jr., "Board of Education and City Hall at Odds Over Money, Again," *New York Times*, March 8, 1992.

18. *Tales Out of School*, p. 6.

19. "VCRs for High School Football Cause an Uproar," *The Executive Educator*, March 1992, p. 10.

Chapter Two: Violence and Crime in Schools

1. Bastian and Taylor, 1989 survey titled "School Crime: A National Crime Victimization Survey Report" taken by the Justice Department and reported in May, 1991, the most recent national figures available.

2. "Sixth Annual Poll of School Executives," conducted by *The Executive Educator* and Xavier University, Ohio, *The Executive Educator*, February 1993.

3. From a survey report released in October, 1993, by The Federal Center for Disease Control and Prevention.

4. "For Many Youths, Carrying Knives Helps Fight Fears," *New York Times*, May 23, 1993.

5. "For Many Youths, Carrying Knives Helps Fight Fears."

6. Letter to the editor, *Sesame Street Parents' Guide*, March 1993.

7. *Caught in the Crossfire: A Report on Gun Violence in Our Nation's Schools*, Center to Prevent Handgun Violence (Washington, DC: September 1990, Second Printing May 1992).

8. Hamburger, Tom, "School Violence Common, Data Say," Minneapolis *Star Tribune*, December 17, 1993.

9.   *A Survey of Experiences, Perceptions, and Apprehensions about Guns among Young People in America,* prepared for The Harvard School of Public Health, conducted by LH Research, Inc. in July 1993.

10. *Kids Carrying Guns: Loopholes in State and Federal Firearms Laws,* Legal Action Project, Center to Prevent Handgun Violence, Washington, DC, 1993.

11. Moynihan, Daniel Patrick, "Seat Belts, Bullets, and American Lives," a letter to the *New York Times,* August 17, 1993.

12. "Keep Your Children Safe," pamphlet, American Academy of Pediatrics and Center to Prevent Handgun Violence, 1992.

13. "Keep Your Children Safe."

14. Kellermann and Reay, "Protection or Peril: An Analysis of Firearm-Related Deaths in the Home," *New England Journal of Medicine,* June 12, 1986.

15. "Protection or Peril."

16. I discuss this issue in depth in my article titled "The Gun Next Door," *Parents* Magazine, February 1994.

17. "Teaching the Bill of Rights: The Case of the Second Amendment," Center to Prevent Handgun Violence, November 1991.

18. Telephone interview with Peter Blauvelt, August 6, 1993.

19. Telephone interview with George Butterfield, January 4, 1994.

20. Telephone interview with George Butterfield, August 2, 1993.

21. Simpson, Michael D., "Looking for Trouble," *NEA Today,* October 1992, p. 27.

22. Telephone interview with Peter Blauvelt, August 6, 1993.

23. Carter, Barry, "Evacuation of Newark School Tied to Mace," Newark *Star-Ledger,* October 24, 1992.

24. Telephone interview with Annette Townley, October 18, 1993.

25. From "School Safety Ideas," a public relations release for America's Safe Schools Week, National School Safety Center, 1992.

26. Telephone interview with Peter Blauvelt, August 6, 1993.

27. Telephone interview with Peter Blauvelt, August 6, 1993.

28. *School Safety Check Book* (Malibu: National School Safety Center and Pepperdine University, 1990), p. 113.

29. *School Safety Check Book,* p. 113.

30. Telephone interview with George Butterfield, August 2, 1993.

31. Rapp, Carrington, and Nicholson, *School Crime and Violence: Victims' Rights* (Malibu: National School Safety Center, revised 1992).

32. "Violence and Youth: Psychology's Response," a report by the American Psychological Association's Commission on Violence and Youth, Washington, DC, August 1993.

33. "Violence and Youth: Psychology's Response."

34. National PTA Position Statement on Gangs, adopted by the 1990 Board of Directors.

35. Henneberger, Melinda, "Gang Membership Grows in Middle-Class Suburbs," *New York Times*, July 24, 1993.

36. Fernandez, Joseph, *Tales Out of School* (New York: Little, Brown, 1993), p. 38.

37. Bishop, Katherine, "As Violence Grows, Schools Order Pupils to Dress for Safety," *New York Times*, January 22, 1992.

38. LaPoint, Holloman, and Alleyne, "Dress Codes and Uniforms in Urban Schools," *Education Digest*, March 1993.

Chapter Three: Discipline

1. Raebeck, Barry, "Beyond the Dunce Cap," *Executive Educator*, April 1993.

2. Telephone interviews with George Butterfield and Peter Blauvelt, August 2 and 6, 1993. Also, as noted in Editors of Data Research, Inc., *1993 Deskbook Encyclopedia of American School Law* (Rosemount, MN: Data Research, Inc., 1993): "School districts and colleges have the power to control student behavior through the use of disciplinary suspensions and expulsions" (p. 136) and "Where state law permits, courts generally uphold the reasonable application of punishment and have been reluctant to find that such punishment violates student due process rights" (p. 133).

3. *1993 Deskbook Encyclopedia of American School Law* .

4. "Putting Away the Paddle—Corporal Punishment in the Schools," *Nuts & Bolts*, project guidelines to help PTAs (Chicago, IL: National PTA Program Division, 1991).

5. *1993 Deskbook Encyclopedia of American School Law* .

6. "Corporal Punishment Factsheet," National Coalition to Abolish Corporal Punishment in Schools, Columbus, OH, April 1993.

7. "Corporal Punishment Factsheet."

8. "Corporal Punishment Factsheet."

9. "Getting Corporal Punishment Banned in Your School District," a pamphlet created to accompany the video, "Changing School Board Policy: Corporal Punishment." National Coalition to Abolish Corporal Punishment in Schools, Columbus, OH; not dated.

10. Telephone interview with Nadine Block, June 16, 1993.

Chapter Four: Arrivals and Departures

1. Telephone interview with Arthur Yeager, August 5, 1993.

2. Telephone interview with Nancy Bauder, September 26, 1991.

3. Editors of Data Research, Inc., *1993 Deskbook Encyclopedia of American School Law* (Rosemount, MN: Data Research, Inc., 1993).

4. "Pedestrian Safety" document, National Safety Council, not dated.

5. deCourcy Hinds, Michael, "Volunteers Line 'Safe Corridor' for Schoolchildren," *New York Times*, November 27, 1993.

6. "Review of Child Identification Systems," resolution adopted by the 1987 convention delegates, National PTA.

7. Hoff, Patricia, "Parental Kidnapping" (handbook), National Center for Missing and Exploited Children, Arlington, VA, August 1988.

8. Carter, Barry, "Law Called Safety Success—Helmets Cited as Kids' Deaths from Bike Accidents Drop," Newark *Star-Ledger*, June 27, 1993.

9. Sacks *et al.*, "Bicycle-Associated Head Injuries and Deaths in the United States from 1984–1988," *Journal of the American Medical Association*, December 4, 1991, and "Bicycle Injury Factsheet," National Safe Kids Campaign, May 1991.

10. Telephone interview with June Million, August 26, 1993.

Chapter Five: Supervision

1. "School Liable for Student's Death Following Warning Not to Step on Skylight," *Legal Notes for Education*, July 1992; "Student Awarded Trial in Negligent Supervision Case," *Legal Notes for Education*, June 1992.

2. "Schools and Courts," *NEA Today*, December 1991.

3. Telephone interview with Michael Imber, May 10, 1993.

4.   Schimmel, David, and Fischer, Louis, *Parents, Schools, and the Law* (Columbia, MD: National Committee for Citizens in Education, 1987), pp. 105–106.

5.   Pellegrini, A.D., "Outdoor Recess: Is It Really Necessary?," *Principal* Magazine, May 1991.

6.   Telephone interview with Annie Barclay, July 7, 1993.

7.   Telephone interview with George Butterfield, August 2, 1992.

8.   "Set Straight on Bullies" brochure, National School Safety Center, not dated.

9.   "Set Straight on Bullies."

10. Information about suicide was gathered during my research and added to the NSSC conclusions.

11. Patel and Plank, "Are Most Field Trips a Waste of Time?" *NEA Today*, June 1986.

12. Schemo, Diana, "School Copes with Shock After Crash," *New York Times*, April 13, 1993.

13. Lynwander, Lynda,"On School Trips, Contracts Allow Searches for Alcohol," *New York Times*, April 7, 1991.

14. Cohen, Robert, "Crime Mars Atlantic Students' Smithsonian Trip," Newark *Star-Ledger*, June 7, 1992.

15. Wilkerson, Isabel, "Michigan Parents Worry Over Children on Snowy Outing," *New York Times*, March 16, 1993.

16. "Car Plows Into Children in Tour, Killing One," *New York Times*, April 30, 1993 (Reuters).

17. *Parents, Schools, and the Law*, p. 106.

18. Telephone interview with George Butterfield, August 2, 1993.

19. "School Safety Update," National School Safety Center, September 1992; also Berlonghi, Alexander, "Managing the Risks of School District Special Events," *School Business Affairs*, June 1991.

Chapter Six: The Building and the Playground

1.   Goodman, Ellen, "Mothers Can't Stave Off the World Forever," syndicated column, Newark *Star-Ledger*, May 8, 1992.

2.   *Schoolhouse in the Red: A Guidebook for Cutting Our Losses* (Arlington, VA: American Association of School Administrators, 1992), p. 8.

3. *Wolves at the Schoolhouse Door: An Investigation of the Conditions of Public School Buildings* (Washington, DC: Education Writers Association, 1989).

4. Kozol, Jonathan, *Savage Inequalities: Children in America's Schools* (New York: Crown, 1991).

5. "Stopping the Countdown," *NEA Today* Educational Support Edition, September 1991.

6. Berger, Joseph, "Report Details School Fraud by Custodians," *New York Times*, November 13, 1992.

7. "Report Reveals Number of Troubling Conditions," Newark *Star-Ledger*, May 4, 1993.

8. Berger, Joseph, "Cleaning Up Abuses: Schools' History Holds Many Clues to a Custodial System Gone Wrong," *New York Times*, November 15, 1992.

9. Telephone interview with George Butterfield, August 2, 1993.

10. Delisle, James R., "Saying 'No' for Safety's Sake," *Gifted Children Monthly*, March 1985.

11. *Handbook for Public Playground Safety* (Washington, DC: U.S. Consumer Product Safety Commission, 1993), p. 20.

12. Telephone interview with John Preston, a mechanical engineer and author of the USCPSC *Handbook for Public Playground Safety*, March 18, 1993.

13. Telephone interview with Doris Cole, June 24, 1993.

14. Goleman, Daniel, "Architects Rediscover the Best City Planners: Citizens," *New York Times*, June 2, 1992.

15. Telephone interviews with Aaron Schwartz,of Perkins, Eastman and Partners architectural firm; Jim Lawler, past president of AIA Institute; and others, January 7, 1993.

Chapter Seven: Physical and Mental Health

1. "Managing Asthma: A Guide for Schools," a guidebook from the National Asthma Education Program at the U.S. Department of Health and Human Services, September 1991.

2. Proctor, Lordi, and Zaeger, *School Nursing Practice: Roles and Standards*, handbook, National Association of School Nurses, Inc., 1993.

3. Telephone interview with Elaine Taboskey, July 7, 1993.

4.   *Digest of Educational Statistics 1992*, Table 91, "Public Elementary and Secondary Schools, by type and size of school: 1990-91," U.S. Department of Education, National Center for Education Statistics, Common Core of Data Survey.

5.   Telephone interview with Annie Barclay, July 7, 1993.

6.   Telephone interview with Annie Barclay, July 7, 1993.

7.   Telephone interview with Elaine Taboskey, July 7, 1993.

8.   "Surgeon General's Report to the American Public on HIV Infection and AIDS," Centers for Disease Control and Prevention, Health Resources and Services Administration, National Institutes of Health, 1993.

9.   "Placement of School Children with AIDS," U.S. Department of Education, Office for Civil Rights, July 1991.

10. "AIDS and the Education of Our Children: A Guide for Parents and Teachers," U.S. Department of Education, May 1988 (the most recent printing as of this writing).

11. Fraser, Katherine, *Someone at School Has AIDS* (Alexandria, VA: National Association of State Boards of Education, 1989).

12. Telephone interview with Elaine Taboskey, July 7, 1993.

13. "Surgeon General's Report to the American Public on HIV Infection and AIDS."

14. Gross, Jane, "Sex Educators for Young See New Virtue in Chastity," *New York Times*, January 16, 1994.

15. "Surgeon General's Report to the American Public on HIV Infection and AIDS."

16. "Records Detail Sex-Abuse by Scoutmasters," *New York Times*, October 15, 1993, p. A18.

17. Leach, Penelope, "How to Protect Your Child against Sexual Abuse," *Parenting* Magazine, September 1991.

18. Schimmel, David, and Fischer, Louis, *Parents, Schools, and the Law* (Columbia, MD: National Committee for Citizens in Education, 1987), p. 115.

19. *Hostile Hallways: The AAUW Survey on Sexual Harassment in America's Schools*, commissioned by the American Association of University Women Educational Foundation, researched by Louis Harris and Associates, June 1993.

20. *Hostile Hallways.*

21. Rubinstein, Carin, "Fighting Sexual Harassment in Schools," *New York Times*, June 10, 1993.

22. Adapted from *Sexual Harassment and Teens: A Program for Positive Change* by Susan Strauss with Pamela Espeland (Minneapolis: Free Spirit Publishing Inc., 1992), p. 16. Used with permission of the publisher.

23. Adapted from *Sexual Harassment and Teens*, page 15, with permission.

24. "Substance Abuse Is Blamed for 500,000 Deaths," *New York Times*, October 24, 1993.

25. "Youths Getting a 'Cheap Thrill' from Inhalants," Newark *Sunday Star-Ledger*, May 2, 1993.

26. "Report to Congress and the White House on the Nature and Effectiveness of Federal, State, and Local Drug Prevention Education Programs," Washington, DC, U.S. Departments of Education and Health and Human Services, October 1987. Reprinted in *Drug Prevention Curricula*, U.S. Department of Education, 1988.

27. Adapted from *Prevention Plus II*, published by the Alcohol, Drug Abuse, and Mental Health Administration, and suggested by the Office for Substance Abuse Prevention and the Department of Education, 1989.

28. *Prevention Plus II*.

29. *Prevention Plus II*.

Chapter Eight: Environmental Issues

1. "Environmental Hazards in Your School: A Resource Handbook," U.S. Environmental Protection Agency, October 1990, p. 2.

2. "The ABC's of Asbestos in Schools," U.S. Environmental Protection Agency, June 1989, pp. 3–4.

3. "The ABC's of Asbestos in Schools."

4. VanDyke, Eric, "Unseen Dangers," *New York Teacher*, the official publication of New York State United Teachers, January 25, 1993.

5. "Unseen Dangers."

6. Acott, Connie, "Why Practice What We Teach?" Colorado Tobacco-Free Schools and Communities Fact Sheet, November 1992.

7. Leary, Warren, "U.S. Ties Second-Hand Smoke to Cancer," *New York Times*, January 8, 1993.

8. Hilts, Philip, "U.S. Issues Guide to Curb Second-Hand Smoke," *New York Times*, July 21, 1993.

9. "In Support of Tobacco-Free School Policies," Colorado Tobacco-Free Schools and Communities, May 1993.

10. "Smoking Policies: Implications for School Administrators," National Association of Secondary School Principals, January 1991.

11. "Eight Steps in Creating a Tobacco-Free School," Colorado Tobacco-Free Schools and Communities, May 1993.

12. Telephone interview with Connie Acott, July 16, 1993.

13. Natale, Jo Anna, "Tainted Water, Poison Paint," *The American School Board Journal*, November 1991.

14. "Results of EPA's National School Radon Survey," EPA Factsheet, not dated.

15. "Congressional Quote of the Month," *NEA Today*, April 1993.

16. "Radon: Testing Your Home for Radon Is Simple," New Jersey Department of Environmental Protection and Energy Radon Program, October 1992.

17. Telephone interview with Dave Mizenko, May 10, 1993.

18. "Contaminated Classrooms: An Investigation of Pest Control Practices," *Public Citizen*, July 1991.

19. "Environmental Hazards in Your School," U.S. Environmental Protection Agency, October 1990

20. *Journal of Pesticide Reform*, a publication of the Northwest Coalition for Alternatives to Pesticides, Winter 1990–1991.

21. Cox, Caroline, and Riley, Becky, "Just Saying No to School Pesticide Use," *Journal of Pesticide Reform*, Winter 1990–1991, and advice from the EPA's pesticide hotline.

22. Brodeur, Paul, *Currents of Death* (New York: Simon & Schuster, 1989).

Chapter Nine: From Classroom to Cafeteria

1. Telephone interview with James Kaufman, July 6, 1993.

2. "Eye Protection in Educational Institutions," New Jersey State Department of Education, 1992.

3. "Laboratory Science," a National Science Teachers Association (NSTA) Position Statement, January 1990.

4. Kaufman, James A., "Home Safe Home," *Science Scope*, November/December 1989.

5.   "What You Need to Know about the Safety of Art and Craft Materials," booklet (Boston: The Art & Craft Materials Institute, not dated).

6.   "Developmentally Appropriate Physical Education Practices for Children," a position statement of the National Association for Sport and Physical Education, 1992.

7.   "Required: Quality, Daily Physical Education," NASPE pamphlet, September 1990.

8.   "Developmentally Appropriate Physical Education Practices for Children."

9.   Telephone interview with Michael Imber, May 5, 1993.

10. "Developmentally Appropriate Physical Education Practices for Children."

11. "Developmentally Appropriate Physical Education Practices for Children."

12. *School Food Service Journal*, June/July 1993.

Chapter Ten: Disaster Preparation

1.   "Guidelines for Emergency Preparedness in Schools," Manitoba Department of Education and Training, Winnipeg, 1991.

2.   "Guidebook for Developing a School Earthquake Safety Program," Federal Emergency Management Agency (FEMA), revised January 1990.

3.   "School Fires Data Package," National Fire Protection Association (NFPA), 1991.

4.   Karter, Michael J., Jr., "NFPA Reports on U.S. Fire Loss—1001," *NFPA Journal*, September/October 1992.

5.   McNeil, Donald G., Jr., "Why So Many More Americans Die in Fires," *New York Times*, December 22, 1991.

6.   Crnkovich, John J., and Dye, Charles M., "Ignorance and Hazards in Academe: The Dilemma of Fire Safety in American Higher Education," an Educational Resources Information Center (ERIC) report, October 19, 1990. ERIC is funded by the U.S. Department of Education.

7.   *Fire in the United States* (Arlington, VA: U.S. Fire Administration, 1993), pp. 151–153, 159, 164.

8.   Telephone interview with Philip Schaenman, July 26, 1993.

9.   Telephone interview with Philip Schaenman, July 26, 1993.

10. Underdue, Towanda, "East Newark School to Add New Lunch Period for Safety," Newark *Star-Ledger,* October 1992.

11. Telephone interview with Bob Brown, July 23, 1993.

Chapter Eleven: Legal Issues

1.   Cells, William 3rd, "Wheelchair Warrior Lays Siege to Schools," *New York Times,* July 28, 1993.

2.   Spivack, Miranda, "The Oprah Bill," *Parenting* Magazine, May 1992.

3.   American Bar Association (ABA), Center on Children and the Law, Criminal History Records Checks, 1991.

4.   Lynwandar, Linda, "Weeding Out Those Unfit for School Jobs," *New York Times,* May 2, 1993.

5.   Spock, Dr. Benjamin, "Family Matters," *Parenting* Magazine, June/July 1993, p. 90.

6.   Berla, Nancy, and Hall, Susan Hlesciak, *Beyond the Open Door: A Citizens Guide to Increasing Public Access to Local School Boards* (Columbia, MD: National Committee for Citizens in Education, 1989).

7.   Schimmel, David, and Fischer, Louis, *Parents, Schools, and the Law* (Columbia, MD: National Committee for Citizens in Education, 1987), p. 120.

Recommended Reading

● Berla, Nancy, and Hall, Susan Hlesciak, *Beyond the Open Door: A Citizens Guide to Increasing Public Access to Local School Boards* (Columbia, MD: National Committee for Citizens in Education, 1989). One of the major obstacles facing parents who want to change school policies is not knowing how to communicate with their local school board. This book details each of the 50 states' school board open meeting laws so parents can gain as much access to the action as possible.

● Editors of Data Research, Inc., *1993 Deskbook Encyclopedia of American School Law* (Rosemount, MN: Data Research, Inc., 1993). Reports from courts regarding actual education law decisions.

● Fancher, Vivian Kramer, *Safe Kids* (New York: John Wiley and Sons, Inc., 1991). Safety at home and around town.

● Fernandez, Joseph, with Underwood, John, *Tales Out of School* (New York: Little, Brown, 1993). A controversial New York City schools chancellor talks about education in the big city.

● Hechinger, Grace, *How to Raise a Street-Smart Child* (New York: Ballantine Books, 1984). Children's safety rules for getting around in large cities.

● Kozol, Jonathan, *Savage Inequalities: Children in America's Schools* (New York: Crown, 1991). An astonishing firsthand look at the deteriorated schools many children must learn in.

● Lewis, Barbara, *The Kid's Guide to Social Action* (Minneapolis: Free Spirit Publishing Inc., 1991). As effective for adults as it is for kids, this book shows concrete ways for one person to really make a difference in government and other social action areas.

● Mann, Stephanie, with Blakeman, M.C., *Safe Homes, Safe Neighborhoods* (Berkeley, CA: Nolo Press, 1993). How to prevent crime in your neighborhood.

● Prothrow-Stith, Deborah, M.D., with Weissman, Michael, *Deadly Consequences* (New York: HarperCollins, 1991). A former Commissioner of Public Health details a plan to reduce teenage violence.

● Schimmel, David, and Fischer, Louis, *Parents, Schools, and the Law* (Columbia, MD: National Committee for Citizens in Education, 1987). A "definitive handbook for parents on the subject of education and the law," as stated in the foreword by Bill Cosby.

● Simmons, J.L., Ph.D., and McCall, George, Ph.D., *76 Ways to Protect Your Child from Crime* (New York: Henry Holt, 1992). Seventy-six short but smart ideas on avoiding crime at home and around town.

● Smith, Dian G., *Raising Kids in a Changing World ("Children's Television Workshop Living Series")* (New York: Prentice Hall Press, 1991). Sensible advice on communicating with children about the risks they face.

● Strauss, Susan, with Espeland, Pamela, *Sexual Harassment and Teens: A Program for Positive Change* (Minneapolis: Free Spirit Publishing, 1992). An interactive program to help teens understand, recognize, and stop sexual harassment. Includes specific recommendations for setting school policy regarding sexual harassment.

Resources

American Academy of Pediatrics
141 Northwest Point Boulevard
P.O. Box 927
Elk Grove Village, IL 60009-0927
Toll-free telephone: 1-800-433-9016
An organization of pediatricians
dedicated to the health and safety
of children. Free catalog of
publications.

American Association of School
Administrators
1801 North Moore Street
Arlington, VA 22209
Telephone: (703) 875-0748
The association for school
administrators. Free catalog.

American Association of Suicidology
2459 South Ash
Denver, CO 80222
Telephone: (303) 692-0985
Provides information about
preventing suicide. Ask for booklet of
publications.

American School Counselor
Association
c/o American Counseling Association
5999 Stevenson Avenue
Alexandria, VA 22304-3300
Toll-free telephone: 1-800-347-6647
The association for professional
counselors. Free resource catalog.

American School Food Service
Association
1600 Duke Street, 7th Floor
Alexandria, VA 22314-3436
Toll-free telephone: 1-800-728-0728
An organization supporting school
food service professionals. Free
catalog.

Art & Craft Materials Institute (ACMI)
100 Boylston Street, Suite 1050
Boston, MA 02116
Telephone: (617) 426-6400
A nonprofit association of
manufacturers of art and craft
materials. Ask for free information
and the booklet, "What You Need to
Know about the Safety of Art & Craft
Materials."

Center for Safety in the Arts
5 Beekman Street
New York, NY 10038
Telephone: (212) 227-6220
A national clearinghouse for research
and education on hazards in the
visual and performing arts, school art
programs, and museums. Ask for their
list of publications.

- Center to Prevent Handgun Violence
  (CPHV)
  1225 Eye Street, N.W.
  Suite 1100
  Washington, DC 20005
  Telephone: (202) 289-7319
  A nonprofit organization helping
  young people and their families
  understand the realities and dangers
  of handgun violence. Free catalog.

- Colorado Tobacco-Free Schools and
  Communities Project
  Colorado State University
  Cooperative Extension
  State 4-H Office
  Aylesworth Hall NW
  Fort Collins, CO 80523
  Telephone: (303) 491-6421
  Free list of publications.

- Federal Emergency Management
  Agency (FEMA)
  P.O. Box 70274
  Washington, DC 20024
  (Do not call)
  Write for a catalog of publications
  titled "The Emergency Preparedness
  Materials Catalog L-164," which
  includes free booklets on disaster
  safety.

- Juvenile Justice Clearinghouse
  National Criminal Justice Reference
  Service
  P.O. Box 6000
  Rockville, MD 20850
  Toll-free telephone: 1-800-638-8736
  Free information about juvenile
  gangs, crime, and juvenile crime.

- Laboratory Safety Workshop
  A National Center for Training and
  Information
  Curry College
  Milton, MA 02186
  Telephone: (617) 333-0500,
  extension 2220
  Conducts a workshop for science
  teachers on lab and other school
  safety, advocates administration
  leadership in safety, and provides
  information on science lab safety to
  the public. Ask for a list of
  publications.

- The National Association for
  Mediation in Education
  University of Massachusetts
  205 Hampshire House
  Amherst, MA 01003
  Telephone: (413) 545-2462
  An association formed to advocate for
  and train schools in mediation
  programs. Ask for a booklet of
  publications.

- National Association for Sport and
  Physical Education
  1900 Association Drive
  Reston, VA 22091-1599
  Telephone: (703) 476-3410
  NASPE is dedicated to strengthening
  basic knowledge about sport and
  physical activity.

- National Association of Elementary
  School Principals
  1615 Duke Street
  Alexandria, VA 22314-3483
  Telephone: (713) 684-3345
  The national association for
  elementary school principals. Free
  catalog.

National Association of Secondary
School Principals
1904 Association Drive
Reston, VA 22091
Toll-free telephone: 1-800-253-7746
The national association for high
school principals. Free catalog of
publications.

National Center for Missing and
Exploited Children
2101 Wilson Boulevard, Suite 550
Arlington, VA 22201
Toll-free telephone: 1-800-THE-LOST
(1-800-843-5678)
Serves as a clearinghouse of
information on missing and exploited
children. Free information and
catalog.

National Clearinghouse for Alcohol
and Drug Information
(Do not write)
Toll-free telephone: 1-800-729-6686
Free books, information, and catalog.

National Coalition to Abolish
Corporal Punishment in Schools
155 West Main Street, Suite 100-B
Columbus, OH 43215
Telephone: (614) 221-8829
Works to eliminate corporal
punishment. Offers free booklet.

National Committee for Citizens in
Education (NCCE)
900 2nd Street, N.E., Suite 8
Washington, DC 20002
Telephone: (202) 408-0447
Promotes the involvement of citizens
in public education. Free catalog.

National Committee for the
Prevention of Child Abuse
200 State Road
South Deerfield, MA 10373-0200
Toll-free telephone: 1-800-835-2671
Works to prevent child abuse in all its
forms. Free catalog.

National Crime Prevention Council
1700 K Street, N.W., 2nd floor
Washington, DC 20006-3812
Telephone: (202) 466-6272
A program funded by the U.S.
Department of Justice that produces
materials to meet the needs of those
working to prevent crime. Free
catalog.

The National Criminal Justice
Reference Service
Juvenile Justice Clearinghouse
P.O. Box 6000
Rockville, MD 20850
Toll-free telephone: 1-800-638-8736
Free information on all aspects of
juvenile crime.

National Fire Protection Association
1 Batterymarch Park
P.O. Box 9101
Quincy, MA 02269-9101
Toll-free telephone: 1-800-344-3555
Free information and catalog on fire
safety materials.

National Information Center
for Children and Youth with
Disabilities (NICHCY)
P.O. Box 1492
Washington, DC 20013
Toll-free telephone: 1-800-695-0285
A national information and referral
clearinghouse that offers free personal
responses and referrals. Free
publications list.

National PTA
700 North Rush Street
Chicago, IL 60611-2571
Telephone: (312) 787-0977
The "National Congress of Parents and Teachers" is the oldest and largest volunteer organization working exclusively on behalf of all children. Free catalog.

National Safe Kids Campaign
111 Michigan Avenue, N.W.
Washington, DC 20010-2970
Telephone: (202) 939-4993
A program of the Children's National Medical Center and Johnson & Johnson aimed at protecting children from unintentional childhood injuries. Facilitates coalition building at a local level. Free catalog.

National Safety Council
1121 Spring Lake Drive
Itasca, IL 60143-3201
Toll-free telephone: 1-800-621-7619
With a mission to protect life and promote health, this organization is a gold mine of information. Ask for the huge General Materials Catalog.

National School Boards Association
1680 Duke Street
Alexandra, VA 22314
Telephone: (703) 838-6722
An association of the members of local school boards. Free catalog.

National School Safety Center
4165 Thousand Oaks Boulevard
Suite 290
Westlake Village, CA 91362
Telephone: (805) 373-9977
An organization formed to promote school safety. Offers many excellent publications. Ask for resources list.

National Youth Sports Foundation
10 Meredith Circle
Needham, MA 02192
Telephone: (617) 449-2499
The National Youth Sports Foundation for the Prevention of Athletic Injuries, Inc. (NYSFPAI) works to promote the safety of children participating in sports.

Northwest Coalition for Alternatives to Pesticides (NCAP)
P.O. Box 1393
Eugene, Oregon 97440
Telephone: (503) 344-5044
Provides a comprehensive information service on the hazards of pesticides and alternatives to their use.

Office on the Americans with Disabilities Act
U.S. Department of Justice
Civil Rights Division
P.O. Box 66118
Washington, DC 20035-6118
Telephone: (202) 514-0301
An information line that answers questions on the ADA and provides free information.

PRIDE
The Hurt Building, Suite 210
50 Hurt Plaza
Atlanta, GA 30303
Toll-free telephone: 1-800-67-PRIDE
(1-800-677-7433)
A private, nonprofit organization devoted to drug abuse prevention through education. Free catalog.

- The Safety Zone
  Hanover, PA 17333
  Toll-free telephone: 1-800-999-3030
  Free catalog of safety products.

- United States Department of
  Education
  (Do not write)
  Toll-free telephone: 1-800-624-0100
  Ask for the free book, "A Parent's
  Guide to Drug Prevention."

- USEPA Public Information Center
  Mail Code 3404
  401 M Street, S.W.
  Washington, DC 20460
  Telephone: (202) 260-7751
  Free information on environmental
  issues address by the United States
  Environmental Protection Agency.

Index

Art class
    building design and
        supply considerations,
        111
    materials and supplies,
        111, 163, 203
    safety in, 163-165
    toxic substances, 164-
        165
Asbestos, 140-142
    defined, 141
    friable, 140, 141
    phase-out regulation,
        141
    safety tips, 141-142
Asbestos Hazard
    Emergency Response Act
    (AHERA), 141
Assault, 41
Asthma, management at
    school, 114
Atmosphere of safety, 7
Attendance, taking, 38

B

Background checks. *See*
    Screening
Band instruments, 165
Barclay, Annie
    on health care in
        schools, 116
    on recess, 84
Bathroom issues. *See*
    Restrooms
Bauder, Nancy, 64
"Beavis and Butthead" (TV
    show), 43
Beepers, 34-35
Before-school activities
    child care, 78-80
    supervision of, 82-83
Behavioral intervention
    techniques, for recess
    aides/supervisors, 84
Bell, Alison, on sex
    education, 124

Berla, Nancy
    on parent involvement,
        7
    on school boards, 201
Bernstein, Fred, on self-
    image, 133
Between Parent and Child
    (Ginott), 46
*Between Parent and
    Teenager* (Ginott), 46
Beyond the Open Door
    (Berla & Hall), 187, 201
Bigotry. *See* Discrimination
Biking to school, 74-75
    and helmets, 74
    rules, 75
Blake, Jeanne, on AIDS,
    120
Blakeman, M.C., on crime
    prevention, 201
Blauvelt, Peter
    on fear, 7, 39
    on knives, 23
    on metal detectors, 33
    on personal defense
        devices, 35
    on reporting violence,
        39
    on school repression of
        safety issues, 14
Bomb threats, 34
Brady Bill, 24
Brady, James, 31
Brady, Sarah, 31
Brainard, Beth, 45
Brodeur, Paul, on EMFs,
    155
Building safety, 95-111
    codes, 110
    maintenance, 96-100
    renovations, 108-109
    See also Architecture
Bullet drills, 94
Bullets. *See under* Guns
Bullying, 84-86
    in bathrooms, 87
    defined, 84

as harassment, 84
    prevention tips, 84-85,
        85-86
Bureau of Alcohol,
    Tobacco and Firearms, 27
Bus safety. *See* School bus
    safety
Bush, George, 27
Butterfield, George
    on bullying, 84
    on calling police, 39, 41
    on closed campus, 31
    on custodians, 97-98
    on locks on lockers, 33

C

Cafeterias
    building design
        considerations, 110
    safety in, 168-170
Caller ID, 34
Carpooling, 72-73
Caught in the Crossfire
    (CPHV), 24, 25
CDC. *See* Centers for
    Disease Control (CDC)
Center for Safety in the
    Arts, 164, 203
Center to Prevent Handgun
    Violence (CPHV), 24, 27
    address and telephone,
        31, 204
    STAR curriculum, 28,
        30-31
Centers for Disease
    Control (CDC), 121
Chained doors, and fire
    safety, 175-176
Chewing tobacco, 147
Child abuse
    corporal punishment,
        as, 60
    prevention of, 205
    See also Sexual abuse

Discipline (Windell), 44

Discrimination, 6, 49-51
activities to discourage, 49-50
and corporal punishment, 60

Disease, transmission of, 122. *See also* specific diseases

Dissing, defined, 47

Dress codes, 52-54. *See also* Uniforms

Drills, conducting, 38

"Drinking Water Coolers That Are Not Lead Free" (EPA), 149

Drugs, 5, 131-137
abuse prevention, 206
abuse signs, 132
cocaine helpline, 133
dealers, and beepers, 34
and guns, 25
information clearinghouse, 132
saying no to, 132-134
school curricula and policies regarding, 134-137
See also Alcohol; Inhalants

Duvall, Lynn, 50

E

Earthquakes, preparing for, 172

"Eddie Eagle" (NRA), 28

Education of the Handicapped Act, 121

Educational Support Employees Association, 84, 116

Edwards, Don, 183

Electrical safety, 96, 111

Electromagnetic fields (EMFs), 155-156

Elementary school principals, association for, 204

Emergency Planning and Community Right-to-Know Information Hotline, 157

Emergency policies, 171-173, 204

"The Emergency Preparedness Materials Catalog L-164" (FEMA), 204

EMFs. *See* Electromagnetic fields (EMFs)

Emotional injury, 6

Emotional problems, and discipline problems, 57

Enrollment capacities, 91

"Environmental Hazards in Your School" (EPA), 158

Environmental issues, 3, 5, 96, 139-158
right-to-know, 157
school involvement, 139-140
in schools vs. homes, 139
See also specific hazards and issues

Environmental Protection Agency (EPA)
address and telephone, 157, 158, 207
on asbestos, 140, 141
on environmental tobacco smoke, 145-146
on hazards in school, 158
on integrated pest management, 153
on lead in drinking water, 148, 149, 150
on pesticides, 153, 154
on radon, 151, 152
on right-to-know, 157

Environmental tobacco smoke (ETS), 145-146

EPA. *See* Environmental Protection Agency (EPA)

Ethnoviolence. *See* Discrimination

Etiquette. *See* Good manners

ETS. *See* Environmental tobacco smoke (ETS)

The Executive Educator magazine, 19

Exploited children. *See* Missing and exploited children

F

Faber, Adele, 46

False enrollment, 181-183

Fancher, Vivian, on safety, 201

Fassler, David, on AIDS, 120

Fear, 7, 39, 69

Federal Emergency Management Agency (FEMA), 172, 173, 204

Federal Emergency Planning and Community Right-to-Know Act (1986), 157

Federal law. *See under* Legal issues

FEMA. *See* Federal Emergency Management Agency (FEMA)

Fernandez, Joseph
on dress codes, 52-53
on education in New York City, 201
on funding, 16
on parent involvement, 10

Festival seating, defined, 93

About the Author

Carol Silverman Saunders has written about safety and health for national magazines including *Good Housekeeping, Parents, Parenting,* and *Sesame Street Parents' Guide.* Her inspiration for this book started when, as a child, she attended unsafe schools in Yonkers, New York. Now, as the chairperson of the PTA safety, environmental, and new playground committees at her children's school, she has initiated many safety improvements. Her goal in life is to help make the world a safer and healthier place for both children and adults.

MORE FREE SPIRIT BOOKS FOR PARENTS

Books on the Move:
A Read-About-It, Go-There Guide to America's Best Family Destinations
by Susan M. Knorr and Margaret Knorr
This one-of-a-kind travel guide describes hundreds of great destinations across the United States—and hundreds of related children's books to read before, during, and after.
368 pp.; illus.; s/c; 6" x 9"
ISBN 0-915793-53-9; $13.95

Bringing Out the Best:
A Resource Guide for Parents of Young Gifted Children
by Jacqulyn Saunders with Pamela Espeland
Hundreds of ways to promote creativity and intellectual development—without pushing. Other topics include how to tell if your child is gifted, what's wrong with "educational" toys, how to choose the right school, how to deal with teachers, how to help your child cope and grow, and more. For parents of children ages 2–7.
240 pp.; illus.; s/c; 7 5/16" x 9 1/4"
ISBN 0-915793-30-X; $12.95

How to Help Your Child with Homework: *Every Caring Parent's Guide to Encouraging Good Study Habits and Ending the Homework Wars*
by Marguerite Radencich, Ph.D. and Jeanne Shay Schumm, Ph.D.
Put an end to excuses and arguments while improving your child's school performance. Realistic strategies and proven techniques make homework hassle-free. Includes handouts, resources, and real-life examples. For parents of children ages 6–13.
208 pp.; illus.; s/c; 7 1/4" x 9 1/4"
ISBN 0-915793-12-1; $12.95

Playing Smart: *A Parent's Guide to Enriching, Offbeat Learning Activities for Ages 4 to 14*
by Susan K. Perry
Hundreds of activities turn spare time into quality time with your child. Topics include gardening, cooking, photography, games, cultural relativity, and more. Most require little preparation; many can be done in small bits of time; all turn learning into play so parents and children enjoy their time together.
224 pp.; illus.; s/c; 7 1/4" x 9 1/4"
ISBN 0-915793-22-9; $12.95

The Survival Guide for Parents of Gifted Kids: *How to Understand, Live With, and Stick Up for Your Gifted Child*
by Sally Yahnke Walker
Up-to-date, authoritative information about giftedness, gifted education, problems, personality traits, and more. Written by an educator of gifted kids and their parents. For parents of children ages 5 and up.
152 pp.; illus.; s/c; 6" x 9"
ISBN 0-915793-28-8; $10.95

Up From Underachievement: *How Teachers, Students, and Parents Can Work Together to Promote Student Success*
by Diane Heacox
Helps students of all ages, with all kinds of school problems. Teachers, students, and parents work together on an Action Plan that spells out everyone's responsibilities. Students are motivated to succeed because they are part of the team.
144 pp.; s/c; 8 1/2" x 11"
ISBN 0-915793-35-0; $14.95

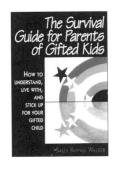

FREE SPIRIT BOOKS FOR YOUNG PEOPLE

Bringing Up Parents:
The Teenager's Handbook
by Alex J. Packer, Ph.D.
Straight talk and specific suggestions
on how teens can take the initiative
to resolve conflicts with parents,
improve family relationships, earn
trust, accept responsibility, and help
create a healthier, happier home
environment. Ages 13 and up.
272 pp.; illus.; s/c; 7 1/4" x 9 1/4"
ISBN 0-915793-48-2; $12.95

*Just Because I Am: A Child's
Book of Affirmation*
by Lauren Murphy Payne, M.S.W.
illustrated by Claudia Rohling
Warm, simple words and gentle,
appealing illustrations strengthen
and support a young child's self-
esteem. Children learn to love,
accept, and respect themselves as
unique individuals. Ages 3-8.
32 pp.; color illus.; s/c; 7 5/8" x 9 1/4"
ISBN 0-915793-60-1; $6.95

Also available:
**A Leader's Guide to Just
Because I Am**
by Lauren Murphy Payne, M.S.W.
and Claudia Rohling
56 pp.; illus.; s/c; 8 1/2" x 11"
ISBN 0-915793-61-X; $12.95

*School Power: Strategies for
Succeeding in School*
by Jeanne Shay Schumm, Ph.D.
and Marguerite Radencich, Ph.D.
Covers getting organized, taking
notes, studying smarter, writing better, following directions, handling
homework, managing long-term
assignments, and more. Ages 11
and up.
132 pp.; illus.; B&W photos; s/c; 8 1/2"
x 11"; ISBN 0-915793-42-3; $11.95

Becoming Myself: *True Stories
About Learning From Life*
by Cassandra Walker Simmons
A T.V. personality and popular
speaker reveals the secrets of her success— self-esteem, strong values, and
a supportive family—in dozens of
true stories about growing up. Her
personal experiences and practical
advice inspire readers to believe in
themselves and be the winners they
are meant to be. Ages 11 and up.
144 pp.; s/c; 5 1/8" x 7 1/2"
ISBN 0-915793-69-5; $4.95

Sofia and the Heartmender
written and illustrated by Marie
Olofsdotter
Beautifully written, exquisitely illustrated, this is the story of a little
girl's search for self-esteem. Sofia's
heart is breaking because the adults
in her life don't understand her. She
goes on a journey in a world of mys-
tery where a wise dog and a gentle
Heartmender help her learn to face
her fears and speak up for herself.
32 pp.; color illus.; h/c; 8 1/2" x 11 1/4"
ISBN 0-915793-50-4; $14.95

*Girls and Young Women
Leading the Way: 20 True
Stories About Leadership*
by Frances A. Karnes, Ph.D.
and Suzanne M. Bean, Ph.D.
These inspiring stories from girls
and young women ages 8 to 21
prove that leadership is for everyone, that leadership opportunities
are everywhere, and that leadership
has many faces and takes many
forms. Ages 11 and up.
168 pp.; B&W photos; s/c; 6" x 9"
ISBN 0-915793-52-0; $11.95

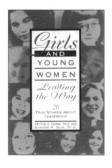

To place an order, or to request a free catalog of SELF-HELP FOR KIDS® materials, write or call:
Free Spirit Publishing Inc.
400 First Avenue North, Suite 616
Minneapolis, MN 55401-1730
toll-free (800)735-7323, local (612)338-2068